I am a student of t____ ____ ____ ____
of God. It is a thr__ ____ ____ ____
torn apart. Ryan LeStrange weaves these three elements together in this insightful book, *The Jochebed
Anointing*—amazing teaching with such a sharp edge
for the days in which we live. I applaud the work of the
Lord through this choice vessel for such a time as this.

—JAMES W. GOLL
FOUNDER, GOD ENCOUNTERS MINISTRIES
AUTHOR, SPEAKER, COMMUNICATIONS TRAINER, AND
RECORDING ARTIST

The keys in this book will help you to navigate the
journey of discovering the call of God for your life.
Ryan has a great revelatory anointing, and this book
will help thousands around the globe to unlock the
destiny inside of them. He is not a colleague to me—
Ryan is family. I want to personally endorse this book
and encourage you to dive into the fresh insight that
Ryan unravels throughout this book.

—JOHN ECKHARDT
BEST SELLING AUTHOR,
PRAYERS THAT ROUT DEMONS

I looked at the title *The Jochebed Anointing* and ques-
tioned, What might this anointing be? I had never
heard of it before. As I began to read Ryan LeStrange's
masterful book on the subject, I couldn't put it down.
I love both the values represented in this book and
the great faith it stirs in the heart. I now am passionate about having the fullness of every aspect of
the Jochebed anointing activated in my life. What is
this Jochebed anointing? Acquire the book and receive

both understanding and the anointing…and then get copies for your friends.

— Dr. Patricia King
Author, Christian Minister, Television Host

Ryan LeStrange's newest release, *The Jochebed Anointing*, is a profound encouragement to mothers, especially those who are first-generation Christians, to be bold and to carry the glory. When you do, your family will be supernaturally impacted for generations to come. And perhaps as a "mother of glory," such as we read of in the lives of Jochebed and Moses, entire nations will be birthed in the glory too.

—Jennifer Eivaz
Founder, Harvest Ministries International
Author, *Seeing the Supernatural* and *Glory Carriers*

THE
JOCHEBED
ANOINTING

RYAN LeSTRANGE

CHARISMA
HOUSE

The Jochebed Anointing by Ryan LeStrange
Published by Charisma House
Charisma Media/Charisma House Book Group
600 Rinehart Road
Lake Mary, Florida 32746

Visit the author's website at www.ryanlestrange.com.

Library of Congress Cataloging-in-Publication Data

Names: LeStrange, Ryan, author.
Title: The Jochebed anointing / by Ryan LeStrange.
Description: Lake Mary, Florida : Charisma House, 2019.
Identifiers: LCCN 2019014528 (print) | LCCN 2019022354 (ebook) | ISBN
  9781629996455 (trade paper)
Subjects: LCSH: Vocation--Christianity. | Jochebed (Biblical figure)
Classification: LCC BV4740 .L47 2019 (print) | LCC BV4740 (ebook) | DDC
  248.4--dc23
LC record available at https://lccn.loc.gov/2019014528
LC ebook record available at https://lccn.loc.gov/2019022354

This publication is translated in Spanish under the title *La unción de Jocabed*, copyright © 2019 by Ryan LeStrange, published by Casa Creación, a Charisma Media company. All rights reserved.

19 20 21 22 23 — 987654321
Printed in the United States of America

I dedicate this book to my soul mate, my friend, my partner, and my forever love, Joy LeStrange. We have had a beautiful and adventurous journey. You have been there for every up and down, every twist and turn. You love me radically, and you make everything about me better. You are my one and only!

CONTENTS

FOREWORD

I AM SO THRILLED to be writing the foreword to this incredible book. I love Ryan LeStrange, and I love everything he invests his time in. He is a profound speaker and is so knowledgeable about almost every spirit you can think of. I've had the honor of working with him, and I don't take that lightly. From the time he told me he was writing on this topic, I knew this book was going to blow away every person who read it—and, boy, was I right!

The Jochebed Anointing will build your faith as it shines light on an amazing woman who, though not well known, was called of God to fulfill an extraordinary purpose. Jochebed gave birth to Moses, the one who led Israel out of slavery in Egypt. Within her womb, she held the answer an entire nation needed.

Jochebed wasn't just a woman of faith—she was a woman of great faith. There's a difference between faith and great faith. Great faith causes us to see miraculous breakthroughs. Jochebed made a tremendous sacrifice to protect her son during a severely adverse time, and she is proof that when you are obedient and willing to sacrifice, God will take care of you. Jochebed gave her son up to be raised by another, but God ultimately gave him back to her. She was still able to nurse Moses and shape him into the world changer he became.

In this book LeStrange shows us that just as God raised up Jochebed, He is raising you and me up to birth great things. Just as He used Jochebed to bring forth something mighty, God will use us, even in our weakness, to showcase His glory. We too can walk in the anointing that was on her life.

One of the things I especially love about this book is that it teaches us that the blessings are in our family line. Jochebed was of the tribe of Levi, meaning she had a priestly lineage. As LeStrange writes, "The Jochebed anointing flows through family. God has chosen the right people to be in your life to unlock your destiny. He has a plan and purpose for both your natural and spiritual family." If God is blessing one, then He has plans to bless the whole natural family and spiritual family.

This book will also make you aware of how important the people are that you keep around you as it reveals mysteries concerning our individual and corporate destiny. It even gives you the characteristics of a world changer and questions at the end of each chapter that can help you begin to walk in this powerful anointing.

I love everything about this book! I know it will take you higher and higher. Get ready to be blessed!

—KIMBERLY JONES-POTHIER (REAL TALK KIM)
CO-PASTOR, CHURCH OF THE HARVEST
AUTHOR, *BEAUTIFULLY BROKEN* AND
WHEN YOUR BAD MEETS HIS GOOD

ACKNOWLEDGMENTS

IT IS IMPOSSIBLE to complete a project like this without help! This message was birthed and first preached in the church of a powerful female leader. I stepped into her building and felt this message bubble up on the inside of me. I had no idea that it would become a full-length book.

Thanks to my editing team, including my mom, Eileen Hromin.

Thanks to my staff, ministry team, volunteers, and partners. Each of you is invaluable. I could never do what I do without your love and dedication. You are gems.

Thank you to Ms. Ronnie Burch, my fiery, firm, kind, and loving spiritual momma. You are a modern-day Jochebed, filled with glory and power. Thank you for your faithful example.

Thanks to my publishers and team at Charisma House.

Finally, thank you to everyone who has faithfully stewarded a call to glory. You are champions, and the world is better because of you.

INTRODUCTION

ONE OF THE primary challenges in life is the quest to find meaning, purpose, and significance. The million-dollar question seems to be, What was I put on earth to do? We all sense something beyond the mundane routines of life. As believers we know we are called to love Jesus and share His love to a lost and dying world. Those are the big pieces of the puzzle, but there is more.

"What is God's master plan for me?" "What am I specifically called to do?" "Whom am I called to do it with?" "Why do things seem to be delayed?" We have all asked these questions at one time or another. It takes a moment to reflect, tune in, and listen to the Father for direction and answers to calm our wandering hearts and minds.

In reality each of us was made for a beautiful and unique purpose. The Creator of heaven and earth crafted each one of us with our distinct quirks, abilities, and talents for His majestic plan. This is the truth concerning our role in God's master plan.

> For your ways are in full view of the LORD, and he examines all your paths.
> —PROVERBS 5:21, NIV

> Know that the LORD is God. It is he who made us, and we are his; we are his people, the sheep of his pasture.
> —PSALM 100:3, NIV

> You are worthy, our Lord and God, to receive glory
> and honor and power, for you created all things, and
> by your will they were created and have their being.
> —Revelation 4:11, niv

Throughout this book we will examine the fascinating life of Jochebed. She was the mother of Moses, one of the Bible's most famous people. In the study of her life are fascinating nuggets of wisdom and the unveiling of mysteries. We will find answers to many of life's questions. We will discover hope and solutions where the enemy has only created and magnified problems.

We will also tap into an unusual anointing and ability. I call it the Jochebed anointing, an anointing to birth the glory and bring deliverance. I call the anointing God's super on our natural. It is His power to fulfill a purpose. This is a vital and powerful anointing. Bondage needs to be broken, assignments need to be fulfilled, and dreams must be realized.

Jochebed was called by God to fulfill an extraordinary purpose: not only the birthing of Moses but also the sacrifice of giving him fully to the Father. Jochebed's womb held the answer to the dilemma of an entire nation. There is a Jochebed anointing for you and me to birth something much greater than we know, to be a part of a bigger story, to endure the wilderness, remain hidden, and then come forth in the glory. Whether you operate with prophetic gifts or not, you will benefit from this book, but I believe every prophetic person needs to read this book and understand the Jochebed anointing.

Jochebed would birth a friend of God! We are being called in this hour to do exploits through *relationship*. God stood before Moses and declared that He knew him and was pleased with him. The reward of surrender is glory and intimacy! God invites you to dream with Him, to build with Him, and to adventure with Him. The Jochebed anointing births friendship and a glory-filled generation.

It is time to unveil the mysteries and birth what heaven has called you to birth. Get ready for a journey deeper into the heart and mysteries of God as we unveil the Jochebed anointing.

> And the Lord said to Moses, "I will do the very thing you have asked, because I am pleased with you and I know you by name."
>
> —Exodus 33:17, NIV

Chapter 1

WHAT IS THE
JOCHEBED ANOINTING?

I WAS HEADING INTO a church to preach as I have done thousands of times. My message was prepared, and I was ready. I had just begun a study on the life of Moses. The Lord had highlighted several things to me. In particular I was drawn to his mother, Jochebed, and the tremendous sacrifice she made to carry, hide, and protect him in the midst of a severely adverse time.

This was all fresh on my mind when I heard the voice of the Lord speak so clearly to me. He said, "I want you to speak on the Jochebed anointing!" The Father has such a sense of humor with me. He seems to love stretching me, surprising me, and causing me to plunge deeper into trusting His plans. This was plainly one of those times.

I laughed and told the Lord I did not have a message on that yet and I really didn't even know what it was. I should not have bothered with that futile argument because as a prophetic person I know better. These are God moments, God opportunities to step out of the boat of comfort and launch into the deep. You cannot be prophetic and play it safe.

Prophetic people know how to move in the *now*. Prophetic people know how to jump in the flow. Prophetic people know how to yield their lips. These experiences bring forth the mind of God and open up mysteries.

One of the Hebrew words for prophet is *nabi*. It means "to bubble forth, as from a fountain...to utter."[1] A vivid picture of this is found in Psalm 45:1, which states: "My heart is overflowing with a good thought; I am speaking my works for the king; my tongue is the pen of a skilled scribe." When the nabi realm opens up, revelation bursts forth, and your tongue takes on prophetic significance.

> But there is a God in heaven who reveals secrets and makes known to King Nebuchadnezzar what shall be in the latter days. Your dream and the visions of your head upon your bed are these.
>
> —DANIEL 2:28

Daniel was functioning in the prophetic realm of dreams and visions. God opened up His hidden wisdom to Daniel to steer and lead a nation. Prophets have answers and insight. The prophetic anointing is one that unravels the mysteries.

It can be scary to your flesh because you launch out past your own limited understanding. You move into the unlimited mind and wisdom of God. Far too many people discount the prophetic anointing and their ability to hear from heaven. It is an anointing to answer the challenges of the day, to answer deep questions and unveil hidden wisdom, to go beyond what has been done before, and to jump in with both feet and dare to believe God.

> He reveals the deep and secret things; He knows what is in the darkness, and the light dwells with Him.
>
> —DANIEL 2:22

...making known to us the mystery of His will, according to His good pleasure, which He purposed in Himself.

—Ephesians 1:9

I learned a long time ago to jump in and trust the Father when He begins to speak. Obedience and daring faith are two key ingredients of the miraculous flow. As He spoke to me that morning about preaching on the Jochebed anointing, I simply said yes. I let God fill my mouth and empower my mind, and I dove headfirst into the nabi realm of bubbling forth.

This message came out of that encounter. God shook me and shook those in attendance as we entered an uncommon realm of glory. Bondage began to melt under the weight of His presence and fire.

GOD MOVES THROUGH FAMILY

Now a man of the house of Levi went and married a daughter of Levi.

—Exodus 2:1

Jochebed was a descendant of the house of Levi. She was married to Amram, and both came from the priestly lineage. God chose them to give birth to a deliverer who would fulfill His promise to set His people free from slavery.

The cries of God's people were coming up before Him. He was preparing an unlikely deliverer and writing a miraculous story of protection, power, and freedom. He had chosen these two vessels to be a part of His miraculous plan.

God uses families for purpose and destiny—including but not limited to natural families. Paul spoke of Timothy as his "true son in the faith" (1 Tim. 1:2). Their relationship shows us that spiritual sons and daughters receive impartation the same way biological sons and daughters do. They receive spiritual gifts and deposits. Timothy would ultimately inherit the apostolic mantle of Paul to lead a powerful church and ministry. This came through family relationship and connection.

The Jochebed anointing flows through family. God has chosen the right people to be in your life to unlock your destiny. God has a plan and purpose for both your natural and spiritual family. God chose the descendants of Levi to fulfill His purpose in the earth.

> "As for me, this is my covenant with them," says the LORD. "My Spirit, who is on you, will not depart from you, and my words that I have put in your mouth will always be on your lips, on the lips of your children and on the lips of their descendants—from this time on and forever," says the LORD.
>
> —ISAIAH 59:21, NIV

> For I will pour water on the thirsty land, and streams on the dry ground; I will pour out my Spirit on your offspring, and my blessing on your descendants. They will spring up like grass in a meadow, like poplar trees by flowing streams.
>
> —ISAIAH 44:3–4, NIV

> The righteous lead blameless lives; blessed are their children after them.
>
> —PROVERBS 20:7, NIV

These verses offer glimpses into the mind of God concerning generational and family blessings. When the Spirit of God moves upon one person in a family, He has plans to move in the *entire* family. There is power in connection. God connects individuals to the right people, family, network, church, or ministry to unlock blessings and potential. There was divine purpose in the lineage of Jochebed! God had major plans for her bloodline.

The devil always tries to block what God has initiated! Much of the warfare over our families is nothing more than a distraction technique. The enemy wants us to be so focused on what he is doing, plotting, and planning that we forget the purposes of God for our families. Again, this is not only natural but also spiritual. The enemy tries to mess with churches and ministries to distract them and divert their purposes. He will sow seeds of strife and division in an attempt to rob the blessing from the house.

Jochebed and Amram, both from the tribe of Levi, had three children: Aaron, Miriam, and Moses. God released three world changers through the loins of this couple. They had a strong anointing to birth deliverance!

GOD MOVES THROUGH FAITH

Jochebed was not just a woman of faith—she was a woman of *great* faith! There is a difference. Great faith empowers miracle breakthroughs. Amram and Jochebed are written about in the Book of Hebrews as examples of great faith. We will examine their mention later in this writing, but I want to focus now on the bold faith they walked in.

We see great faith mentioned by Jesus in the healing of the centurion's servant. This man was a Gentile outside the covenant, yet his faith moved Jesus. His faith not only caused Jesus to pay attention, but it got the answer! Great faith is answered. The centurion understood the rank of Jesus in the spirit and put a demand upon His authority. He understood the power of the

5

spoken word, and he simply requested of Jesus to do what He was authorized to do.

> And when Jesus entered Capernaum, a centurion came to Him, entreating Him, and saying, "Lord, my servant is lying at home, sick with paralysis, terribly tormented."
>
> Jesus said to him, "I will come and heal him."
>
> The centurion answered and said, "Lord, I am not worthy that You should come under my roof. But speak the word only, and my servant will be healed. For I am a man under authority, having soldiers under me. And I say to this man, 'Go,' and he goes, and to another, 'Come,' and he comes, and to my servant, 'Do this,' and he does it."
>
> When Jesus heard it, He was amazed and said to those who followed, "Truly I say to you, I have not found such great faith, no, not in Israel. And I say to you that many will come from the east and west and will dine with Abraham, Isaac, and Jacob in the kingdom of heaven. But the sons of the kingdom will be thrown out into outer darkness. There will be weeping and gnashing of teeth."
>
> Then Jesus said to the centurion, "Go your way. And as you have believed, so let it be done for you." And his servant was healed that very moment.
>
> —MATTHEW 8:5–13

A Roman centurion caused Jesus to marvel. The Roman soldiers were not known to be friendly with the Jews, nor were the Jews fond of the Romans. I have discovered an amazing thing about great faith: it bypasses all limitations, including cultural limitations. It lays hold of the promise of God with no regard for what man deems acceptable.

Growing up as a Roman, this man would have had a pagan background. He was stationed in Palestine to enforce the emperor's government and laws upon the Jewish people. He would have excelled to the level of leadership in the Roman army through brutality. He would not have been a person you would expect to cause Jesus to marvel, and yet he did! This was a foreshadowing of the exact thing Jesus came to do, to tear down the wall of sin and separation so all people can come to salvation. This situation was a demonstration of grace.

I believe the Roman centurion's understanding of the spirit realm is what caused Jesus to marvel at his faith. He knew that whatever Jesus spoke would come to pass. He understood the power of God in action. This was revelation.

Revelation births faith, and faith moves things from one realm into another. To tap into this realm of anointing and glory, it takes uncommonly great faith.

Jochebed and Amram also possessed uncommonly great faith. God chose them to birth a dimension of glory and deliverance for the people of Israel. Their assignment was set against a backdrop of tyrannical rule and fear: heinous persecution against the Hebrew people abounded; Pharaoh threatened and murdered Hebrew children; and demonic bondage overtook the land. The power of God was seemingly absent, and yet God was working!

If you were alive at the time and in the Hebrews' situation, you might have easily felt forgotten. Where was God's promise of deliverance? When would He move? Why did He allow this unfair and unjust rule to continue? These were all relevant questions at that time, but God's hand was moving the puzzle pieces into place to perform a powerful work of deliverance in the land.

God Moves According to His Timing

> So that you may not be lazy, but imitators of those
> who through faith *and patience* inherit the promises.
> —Hebrews 6:12, emphasis added

Prophetic people must understand the critical element of divine timing. Many times we see and speak the promise, yet we don't see it come to pass in the timing we feel or sense. This is where faith and patience are critical. The Jochebed anointing is time-sensitive and must have the fruit of patience at work.

I believe God has already released major movements and deliverance in the realm of the spirit. People are becoming pregnant right now with prophetic vision as God prepares hearts for a surge of His power! He is working behind the scenes, but it will require patience on our part.

The word *patience* means the act of being patient. Let's dig a little deeper to get a clearer picture. According to Webster's online dictionary, *patient* means "bearing pains or trials calmly or without complaint; manifesting forbearance under provocation or strain; not hasty or impetuous; steadfast despite opposition, difficulty, or adversity."[2]

You will need patience to walk in extraordinary faith, to birth realms of uncommon glory, potential, and promise. You must be able to bear pain and trial. Times of conflict and challenge birth the most powerful deliverers. This should give you a different perspective on the presence of difficult circumstances. Often in these moments, God chooses a man or woman to break the cycle.

The Seed Breaks the Cycle

Cycles are broken by seed. Moses, the seed of deliverance, was entrusted to Jochebed and Amram. God could have chosen any two people alive at that time to birth, guide, pray for, and protect this valuable seed, but He chose them.

Even now God is choosing people to carry cycle-breaking seeds, to cultivate answers and solutions, to receive heavenly downloads and ideas that will shift culture, and to build outreaches, churches, ministries, businesses, and organizations. He is planting wild dreams in the hearts of daring men and women—globe-trotting missions in the hearts of yielded vessels and game-changing economic strategies in the minds of the imaginative and willing. He is establishing people in the earth to manifest the kingdom and to rule and reign.

It is a mystery, but great things in the kingdom begin small! They start as an idea, an unction, a vision, or a dream. This is the essence of a seed—a seemingly little thing with massive potential. That tangible expression of the mind of God is a glimpse into the possibilities of the unlimited One!

> For God speaks once, yes twice, yet man does not perceive it. In a dream, in a vision of the night, when deep sleep falls upon men, in slumber on their beds, then He opens the ears of men, and seals their instruction.
>
> —Job 33:14–16

Several prophetic dimensions revealed in the life of Jochebed apply to us. Jochebed's destiny was great and her obedience fierce. This speaks to us today!

Each of us has been handpicked by God for a unique and timely work in the earth. It all comes down to our level of obedience. We cannot delegate our obedience to another or blame adversity for our lack of cooperation with the plans of God. In this very moment I believe God is looking for a Jochebed generation who will rise and launch into each changing realm of glory and destiny.

> If you are willing and obedient, you shall eat the good
> of the land.
>
> —ISAIAH 1:19

Obedience is critical in fulfilling personal and corporate destiny. When we obey God, we enjoy His blessings. Obedience can be costly and cause us to do things that are uncomfortable, but it is all part of God's master plan.

Obedience is the fruit of surrender. When I am surrendered to the will of the Father, I am happy to follow His instructions even when I don't understand. This comes as I plant my life in prayer. Prayer is that time of reflection and balance. I come into His presence with questions, and as I quiet my mind, my spirit begins to receive instruction from my Father. His voice calms the storm and brings divine peace.

In His presence I am empowered to live boldly. I am free from the fear of man and ready to launch forth into His plan. This is the journey of obedience. It is fueled by hunger and desire to please the Father. The world cannot understand it because it is the mark of a disciple. An obedient one has yielded to the discipline of the Father, denying his own desire, to fulfill His will. The rewards far outweigh the price.

> My responsibility is to obey, to surrender my heart and
> to yield myself to the will of God. It is in the process
> of obedience that we gain understanding. You can't get
> the peace that passes understanding until you give up
> your right to understand.[3]
>
> —BILL JOHNSON

The mysteries of the Jochebed anointing center on two dramatic themes in her life. These themes are glory and deliverance. The Jochebed anointing unlocks glory (the presence of God) and births deliverance. It holds a level of freedom that breaks people out of bondage.

CHARACTERISTICS OF WORLD CHANGERS

Jochebed displayed some essential characteristics for every world changer.

- **Bravery.** The Jochebed anointing is one of supernatural bravery. She was fearless in the midst of a death decree. She defied the instructions of an evil ruler to obey the will of heaven. The Jochebed anointing causes you to stand up when hell is screaming at you to sit down.

- **Family destiny.** As we have already described, this is a family anointing! God's plans are generational, and the life of this woman affirms that reality.

- **Commitment.** This is the difference maker. Jochebed could have folded under pressure at several key points, but she did not. She had supernatural strength and commitment. She did not back down from God's direction, and neither can you!

- **Great faith.** People of great faith are people of great exploits! They shake nations and generations. The Jochebed anointing partners with the spirit of faith to get the job done.

- **Patience.** She did not get weary! Demons try to make you weary. They try to outlast you, but the realm of God's glory (His presence) will uphold you and refresh you.

- **Birthing.** Everything in the kingdom must be birthed! We are called to birth ministries, visions, plans, exploits, and legacies. The Jochebed anointing births things into the earthly realm by praying, decreeing, standing, sowing, and warring.

- **A seed of miracles.** Seeds produce harvest. We must have twofold faith: faith to sow and faith to receive!

- **Endurance.** Jochebed went the distance. God is not anointing a generation to be great starters. He is anointing us to complete the mission! He wants us to make it to the end with joy and strength.

- **Unwavering trust.** To fulfill her mandate, Jochebed had to trust God deeply. She was not moved by attacks, lies, or temporary challenges. God is raising up a generation whose trust is in Him. They will not back down when He speaks.

The Mantles of Moses

Jochebed birthed Moses, who would fulfill the promise of God to the people of God. He was chosen by God to embark on an apostolic mission. The word *apostle* means a sent one. Apostles are sent to a people, a place, a region, or a group. Moses was sent with a mandate to liberate Israel. He was God's chosen man for the time of deliverance.

Though the office of the apostle did not come into fruition until the church was established, I believe Moses was an Old Testament type of apostle. He served in an apostolic capacity. In fact God Himself described Israel under Moses' leadership as the church in the wilderness.

This is he, that was in the church in the wilderness
with the angel which spake to him in the mount Sina,
and with our fathers: who received the lively oracles to
give unto us.

—ACTS 7:38, KJV

Moses was, in many ways, also a prophet. He had a unique
face-to-face relationship with God. I would use the term *hybrid*
to describe his dual function.

The LORD spoke to Moses face to face, just as a man
speaks to his friend. When he returned to the camp,
his servant Joshua, the son of Nun, a young man, did
not depart from the tent.

—EXODUS 33:11

Prophets are people of intimacy. The prophetic ministry is
one of intimacy and revelation. Prophets see, know, hear, and
speak. They have the testimony of Jesus.

I fell at his feet to worship him. But he said to me,
"See that you not do that. I am your fellow servant,
and of your brothers who hold the testimony of Jesus.
Worship God! For the testimony of Jesus is the spirit
of prophecy."

—REVELATION 19:10

At the most potent levels of function, the prophetic ministry
draws people back to the heart of Jesus. Prophets have a way of
cutting through all the clutter and revealing the heart of Jesus
to the people of God. Prophets also challenge wicked systems
and are powerful spiritual warriors. Prophets cast out demons
and tear down demonic altars.

> See, I have this day set you over the nations and over
> the kingdoms, to root out and to pull down, to destroy
> and to throw down, to build and to plant.
>
> —Jeremiah 1:10

Jeremiah was called as a prophet to root out, to pull down, to destroy, and to throw down! All those things had to happen before the building and planting could have full impact. This is why the apostolic and prophetic offices are linked together, along with the teacher, as foundational to the church. The prophets speak the heard things. They expose the hidden demons. The prophets receive revelation of what needs to change, what God wants to do, and His heart behind it. Apostles come in with a grace to strategically build and plant by the leading of the Spirit of God.

> …having been built upon the foundation of the apos-
> tles and prophets, Jesus Christ Himself being the chief
> cornerstone.
>
> —Ephesians 2:20

God sent Moses along with Aaron and Miriam as prophets. There was a synergy of the two anointings of prophet and apostle. The Jochebed anointing contains both the apostolic and prophetic dimension.

The apostolic brings governing (kingdom enforcement and authority), liberty (bondage broken), and building to establish the rule of Christ! Apostles are direct ambassadors of Jesus Christ and His glory. The apostolic anointing is a Jesus-revealing anointing.

The prophetic brings forerunning (out ahead in seeing, knowing, and hearing), intimacy (praying, seeking, and pursuing), seeing (wondrous dreams, visions, and prophetic encounters), and speaking (releasing the voice of the Lord).

In no way is this a complete list of all the attributes of these various anointings or offices. It is a partial, quick overview of the story of Jochebed and Moses and the truths we are examining prophetically in this writing. Volumes could not contain all the wonderful attributes of the various gifts and offices of Christ and His church.

Finally, Jochebed's anointing represents a rich and beautiful glory that births deliverance. Moses led a movement surrounded by the glory of God and directed through His magnificent presence. Deliverance sprang forth from the glory! This is a thesis that runs throughout this prophetic picture. Majestic freedom occurs supernaturally in the glory realm.

We often learn and study the principles of deliverance, which we should, but there is another level available! There is a deliverance element to the glory. When God's weighty presence permeates the atmosphere, demonic powers are brought low. This is true in the lives of individuals, ministries, regions, and territories. We will unveil many mysteries as we dig deeper into the prophetic picture of the Jochebed anointing.

PROPHETIC PRAYER

Lord, I pray that I am always ready to step out of the boat for moments with You. I decree that I flow in the prophetic and have prophetic dreams and visions, unraveling mysteries. Let my family fulfill their purpose and destiny. I decree that my bloodline is mighty on this earth, and no weapon formed against us will prosper! I pray that I walk in uncommon faith and plant uncommon seeds to birth uncommon miracles, in the name of Jesus. Amen.

MY DECREE OVER YOU

I decree that you and your family are warriors, you are descendants of royal blood, and you have a lineage of faith. I decree that you are able to withstand trials, you are brave and committed, and you have patience and faith to birth spiritual encounters and realms of glory. You were born to birth greatness!

POINTS TO CONSIDER

- Do I surrender and yield myself daily to the will of God?
- Do I have the level of faith to endure pressure?
- Am I able to trust God in the midst of negative reports?
- Do I have faith to sow and then to receive?
- Do I really believe that I can change a generation?
- Have I sacrificed and paid the price to birth my destiny?

Chapter 2

THE MYSTERY OF HONOR

M ANY PEOPLE DO not understand the correlation between honor and the glory of God. God's glory unlocks revelation, promotion, healing, and favor. A study of the life of Moses reveals a man with unusual dimensions of God's glory on his life. He was mantled in the glory. He became caught up in the glory of God and was known as a friend of God. By the glory, God led the children of Israel out of bondage.

Conversely, honor is connected with humility and will require you to take the *low* road. Based on the meanings of these two words, you can see how it might be easy to miss the connection between honor and the glory. In many ways they seem like opposites.

In the midst of honor the plans of the Lord are secured in your life. This is one of the great paradoxes of the kingdom. How can I choose a seemingly lower road and yet rise under the winds of God? How can I take the long path and end up passing those who fought and clawed for their promotion? The answer is simple: it is the mystery of honor. Honor and God's glory serve together as promoters in the kingdom. As you honor God by putting Him first, endeavoring to walk in His ways and refusing to leave the path He has you on, your blessing and promotion will come forth.

It is, in many ways, a backward kingdom. You sow, and then

you reap. The first are last, and the last are first. You give your life away, only to discover a brand-new life. These steps cannot be taken by a fleshly man or woman yielding to destructive appetites. The road of honor can only be navigated with and through the mind of Christ. Actualizing a life of honor *requires* the presence of God.

Jochebed was a woman whose destiny was intertwined with honor and the glory. Her name literally means honor of God or God is glory. She was a woman of honor who carried and birthed a man of glory because she honored the law of God above the law of man. In fact she risked everything to pursue God's plan for her life.

THE REWARDS OF HONOR

Jochebed ultimately put God and His plan first. She risked her life to honor the plans of God. She laid it all on the line. She set her own well-being aside. In the midst of her honor for God and His plans, His glory came and acted as her covering. Not only was God's glory with her but also her acts of honor invited uncommon realms of glory to overshadow her son. When we walk in honor, God's glory is our reward. When we honor God, our obedience secures dimensions of His glory for our family. He is a generational promise keeper! Out of the midst of honor God's glory arises, and His majesty is unfolded. God wants to take you down a seemingly inconvenient road so you can discover parts of His uncommon goodness for your life.

> He who follows after righteousness and mercy finds life, righteousness, and honor.
> —PROVERBS 21:21

Following Jesus' footsteps empowers a life of honor. As we walk in godly honor, we place a higher value on God's ideas and His agenda than on our own. Surrender is the fruit of time spent in the presence of God. To put this in simple terms, as believers we are the walking dead, totally surrendering our lives to His plan.

According to Romans, we are to be living sacrifices. The sacrifice in the Old Testament was offered to God to unlock a sweet aroma of surrender. It was to atone for the sins of the people. We know that Jesus came and shed His blood to eradicate the grip of sin and death! He came to heal, save, free, and redeem.

> But Christ, when He came as a High Priest of the good things to come, by a greater and more perfect tabernacle, not made with hands, that is to say, not of this creation, neither by the blood of goats and calves, but by His own blood, He entered the Most Holy Place once for all, having obtained eternal redemption. For if the blood of bulls and goats, and the ashes of a heifer, sprinkling the unclean, sanctifies so that the flesh is purified, how much more shall the blood of Christ, who through the eternal Spirit offered Himself without blemish to God, cleanse your conscience from dead works to serve the living God?
> —HEBREWS 9:11–14

He was the sacrifice for sinful humanity. His act of love empowers us to be living sacrifices. What if our lives became a sweet smell in heaven? What if we emitted an incense of love and surrender?

For we are to God a sweet fragrance of Christ among
those who are saved and among those who perish.

—2 CORINTHIANS 2:15

As living sacrifices our surrender is ascending to the throne
of God. Our submission is an act of honor. We must regu-
larly contend against two forces: the temptation of our adversary the devil and the works of the flesh, which are rooted in
carnal and ungodly appetites. These two forces can be overcome
by walking in the Spirit. As we spend quality time in the presence of God, our spirit man strengthens and the flesh weakens.
The Spirit of God empowers us to live in a place of sacrificial
honor, and we lose our lives only to find His! This is one of the
enigmas of honor.

He who finds his life will lose it, and he who loses his
life for My sake will find it.

—MATTHEW 10:39

For if you live according to the flesh, you will die, but
if through the Spirit you put to death the deeds of the
body, you will live.

—ROMANS 8:13

THE NATURE OF HONOR

What is honor? According to Webster's, the noun *honor*
means "a good name or public esteem; a showing of usually
merited respect; privilege;…one whose worth brings respect
or fame;…an evidence or symbol of distinction: such as…an
award."[1]

As a verb *honor* means "to regard or treat (someone) with
admiration and respect: to regard or treat with honor; to give

special recognition to: to confer honor on; to live up to or fulfill the terms of [as in] *honor* a commitment."[2]

Giving is a manifestation of honor. When we honor something, we place value upon it. When we honor the presence of God, we are willing to rise early and stay up late to seek Him. Honor is manifested by pursuit. People are willing to pursue what they honor.

I know people who have expensive hobbies. They are willing to save up their money, travel, sacrifice, and spend time away from their family just to enjoy their hobbies. They are willing to pay for something that they have placed value upon.

> Honor the LORD with your substance, and with the first fruits of all your increase; so your barns will be filled with plenty, and your presses will burst out with new wine.
>
> —PROVERBS 3:9–10

The word here for *honor* is the Hebrew word *kabed*. It means to be heavy, weighty, grievous, hard, rich, honorable, glorious, burdensome, honored, made heavy or abundant, or to enjoy honor.[3]

The Lord is speaking of weighty dimensions of honor. It is a weighty thing to honor God and put Him first in our finances. It moves beyond our mere words and demonstrates a level of serious commitment to the Lord. Imagine weighty, heavy giving! Imagine giving that shocks the minds of other people. This is the realm described here.

This is part of the mystery of honor and favor. Giving and sowing release uncommon levels of increase and favor. Think about it for a moment: the children of Israel came out of Egyptian bondage loaded down with heavy blessings. This was in a period of history before cash currency. They were physically carrying the weight of gold, silver, and precious metals.

God wants to bring us into a place of weighty giving, weighty honor, weighty glory, and weighty promotion. Honor unlocks realms of promotion no man can block—weighty realms where the blessings of God overtake you.

When we give, we are expressing honor. Giving and generosity will bring glory on the scene. I have found that those with a stingy mindset are dry. They are often under the influence of a religious spirit. In fact I have never ministered in a religious church where people loved giving and talking about generosity. Some religious churches will give to charity and help their community, but they get upset if you really begin to advocate radical giving and generosity. It causes the spirit of religion to manifest.

Where the spirit of religion rules, the message of giving is opposed. Religious people cannot comprehend the tender and loving nature of the Father's immense heart toward His children, partially due to the mindset of shame, bitterness, and condemnation associated with the religious spirit.

> Every good gift and every perfect gift is from above
> and comes down from the Father of lights, with whom
> is no change or shadow of turning.
> —James 1:17

God does not have bad gifts to give us! He gives only good and perfect gifts. He gives gifts that bless our lives. This is the expressed love of a good, good Father.

> But You, O Lord, are a God full of compassion and gracious, slow to anger, and abundant in mercy and truth.
> —Psalm 86:15

A new commandment I give to you, that you love one
another, even as I have loved you, that you also love
one another.

—JOHN 13:34

In these verses we catch a glimpse into God's massive heart
of love toward us. He is full of compassion and grace. He
challenges us to love one another even as He has loved us.
His love is not passive! It is expressed by the act of sacrifice at
Calvary. He lavishes His sacrificial love upon us and gives us
a new nature whereby we can love others by the power of His
Spirit working in us and through us.

Jesus was willing to face the cross because He deemed us
worthy. The devil still fights this revelation today. He is still
lying and trying to talk humanity into believing that they are
dishonorable and worthless. Yet the Bible teaches us that God
found such value in us that He gave His best. He placed honor
upon our lives, upon our destinies, and upon our salvation.

Honor empowers giving. When you honor someone, you
celebrate them with gifts. In the kingdom these principles are
directly related. We demonstrate honor through generosity.
This is an often-overlooked principle because of Western culture
and religious teaching.

People without honor refuse to give into the lives of those
who have blessed and helped them. Dishonorable people do not
walk in integrity toward the Lord in the area of giving. Think
about it for a moment: placing value on a person or thing is
a dimension of honor. We will pay a high price for things we
value. I can think of certain fashion brands that use similar
materials as other brands, but because of the exclusivity of their
brand and the reputation of their designers, people are willing
to pay a higher price.

Let the elders who rule well be counted worthy of double honor, especially those who labor in the word and doctrine. For the Scripture says, "You shall not muzzle the ox that treads out the grain," and, "The laborer is worthy of his reward."

—1 Timothy 5:17–18

In this passage Paul is teaching Timothy about governing the church and dealing with people. He is advocating the financial blessing of the elders who teach and feed the flock of God. He is making a correlation between giving and honor. When we value leaders, we will sow into their lives and leadership. This is the conferring of honor.

This is foreign to the dishonorable who are easily angered by the concept of giving to demonstrate gratitude and support of another. The Bible teaches us that where our treasure is, our heart will be also (Matt. 6:21). This means that natural gifts, money, and resources reflect our priorities. Most dishonorable people are dishonorable in the area of giving.

- They sow insignificant seeds and want a significant harvest.

- They don't support the vision to which they profess connection.

- They do not bless those who are gifts in their lives.

- Often, rather than support and bless, they hinder and complain.

Dishonorable people will reap a toxic harvest if they do not repent and change course.

> Be not deceived. God is not mocked. For whatever a
> man sows, that will he also reap.
>
> —GALATIANS 6:7

This is one of the chief laws of the kingdom: the law of sowing and reaping. Paul is teaching here on the principle of sowing into the flesh or sowing into the kingdom. Sowing into the flesh will bring forth a corrupt harvest of destruction and defeat. Sowing into the realm of the Spirit will bring transformation and breakthrough.

Honor requires discipline. Honorable people do not just succumb to the voice or dictates of their flesh. They have chosen to put God first and live surrendered even while it is difficult. They are determined to pursue an uncommon path. Dishonorable people yield to the ungodly appetites of their flesh.

As a student preparing for ministry, I remember hearing one of my mentors share a personal experience of heartbreaking betrayal. A member of my mentor's staff had left in a very public and nasty way. In the departure this person took people from the ministry of my mentor to launch a new ministry in the same town. The intent and the method showed no respect or honor; it was decidedly dishonorable.

This person's new ministry seemed to be growing, and people were coming. The ministry of my mentor seemed to be suffering. I voiced my concern to my mentor, but he spoke powerful wisdom into my life. He taught me that the foundation of a thing is critical. He said that everything in the kingdom will be submitted to the laws of the kingdom, and he told me that time would judge the matter. He also said such things may look and seem good for a time, but eventually their dishonor would demand a harvest.

This was a treasured lesson and an enduring perspective for a hungry, young leader like me. I watched over a period of years as the rogue ministry fell apart piece by piece. Now that I am older and wiser, I can look back and clearly see that the ministry was a league of dishonorable people! Dishonorable people are not loyal or committed. They are in it for what they can get out of it; they will turn on a leader in a moment. You cannot build anything significant with dishonorable people. They will eventually turn against you. They are more united in their envy, jealousy, and works of the flesh than in a vision or purpose. A ministry led by people like this is built on a faulty foundation.

> Who is wise and understanding among you? Let him show his works by his good life in the meekness of wisdom. But if you have bitter envying and strife in your hearts, do not boast and do not lie against the truth. This wisdom descends not from above, but is earthly, unspiritual, and devilish. For where there is envying and strife, there is confusion and every evil work.
>
> But the wisdom that is from above is first pure, then peaceable, gentle, open to reason, full of mercy and good fruits, without partiality, and without hypocrisy. And the fruit of righteousness is sown in peace by those who make peace.
>
> —JAMES 3:13–18

Let me interject here that we all begin as dishonorable people because we simply don't know better. We are typically operating in carnal wisdom that lacks love and integrity until we receive the wisdom God provides from above.

> The fear of the LORD is the instruction of wisdom, and before honor is humility.
>
> —PROVERBS 15:33

Humility comes before honor. Acts of dishonor are connected to pride. Pride is the exaltation of self. The prideful are self-serving, self-loving, self-promoting, and self-protecting. The humble have decided to submit their ways to the Lord. Humility is a manifestation of surrender in the kingdom.

Worship is an expression of honor! True worship is a demonstration of surrender. This is why we lift our hands, bow, and lay before the Lord. We are physically demonstrating what is already real in the realm of the Spirit.

> Lord, you are my God. I honor you and praise you, because you have done amazing things. You have always done what you said you would do; you have done what you planned long ago.
> —Isaiah 25:1, ncv

When I give God my offering of worship, I am honoring Him. I am remembering what He has done for me. I am lifting His name high and celebrating who He is. Honorable people love to worship. God's glory and honor are connected by worship. You cannot live honorably without surrender. Worship is one of the best demonstrations of surrender in the life of a believer.

> David danced before the Lord with all of his might, and he wore a linen ephod. So David and the whole house of Israel escorted the ark of the Lord with shouting and the sound of the horn.
> —2 Samuel 6:14–15

I love this picture of David as the king of Israel becoming undignified in the presence of God. He didn't care about his title, his stature, or his position! He wanted the glory. He was dancing from a place of absolute, childlike adoration. This is worship at its pinnacle. It is wild, messy, undignified, and radically thankful. This is surrendered worship that honors God above all others!

> So David said to Michal, "It was <u>before the Lord,</u> <u>who chose me</u> instead of your father and all his house, to appoint me ruler over the people of the Lord, over Israel. Therefore I will play music before the Lord. And I will be even more undignified than this, and will be humble in my own sight. But as for the maidservants of whom you have spoken, by them I will be held in honor."
>
> Therefore Michal the daughter of Saul had no children to the day of her death.
>
> —2 Samuel 6:21–23, nkjv

David's wife Michal was offended by his passionate adoration of the Father. She was embarrassed. He was lavishing his praise and thanks on God with no concern for man's opinion. This is the mark of a free man or woman! They simply do not value the opinion of man above the presence of God.

David's worship was the ultimate manifestation of honor for his Father. When challenged by his wife, he boldly professed that he would become even more undignified. He had a goal in mind. He wanted to get so lost in the presence of God that every shred of self-preservation and pride was banished from his life. He knew that God had lifted him, mercifully forgiven him, and miraculously chosen him, and he refused to live like an orphan when he was called to be a son.

Michal dishonored the presence of God and was made barren. Dishonorable people will not birth the fullness of that which God has called them to birth. Worshippers are fruitful. Worshippers conceive, carry, and deliver the seeds of destiny.

Kingdom mandates are released and produced in the midst of honor and glory.

Honorable people submit to authority and embrace kingdom protocol.

> Let every person be subject to the governing authorities. For there is no authority except from God [granted by His permission and sanction], and those which exist have been put in place by God. Therefore whoever resists [governmental] authority resists the ordinance of God. And those who have resisted it will bring judgment (civil penalty) on themselves.
> —ROMANS 13:1–2, AMP

THE NECESSITY OF KINGDOM PROTOCOL

All too often in Charismatic circles people develop poor attitudes toward leadership and ministry gifts. They form an unscriptural idea that any realm of authority is evil. This comes from abusive, controlling leadership and improper teaching. Every believer is equal at the cross as a son or daughter of God. This is a theological truth based upon the Word of God. Another spiritual reality we must acknowledge is the various assignments, ranks, positions, and roles within the kingdom of God and the body of Christ.

Apostles, prophets, pastors, teachers, and evangelists have been given places of authority as gifts given to the body of Christ. They are equipped by God to lead and govern within their jurisdiction. Kingdoms have protocols. For example, there is a protocol if you are invited to see the royal family of England. There is a protocol if you visit the president of the United States. There are biblical protocols concerning prayer, giving, worship, and the laws of the kingdom.

According to Webster's, the word *protocol* means "a code prescribing strict adherence to correct etiquette and precedence (as in diplomatic exchange and in the military services)."[4] To bring this into proper understanding, the kingdom of God has laws and a culture. There is a proper administration of spiritual gifts, offices, and mechanisms. While there is proper administration, there is also improper administration. Interestingly, in Paul's instruction on the nine gifts of the Spirit in 1 Corinthians 12, the word *administrations* is mentioned. People can have the right gift and the right heart but <u>breach</u> kingdom protocol and create a mess.

Many of our churches do not go deep in teaching protocol because they have become babysitting centers instead of places of equipping. When you fail to honor kingdom protocol, you are in a breach! When the order of the kingdom is violated, you might fail to get proper results or even open yourself up to deception. Believers should be appreciative of teaching and instruction on kingdom operations—how to flow in the spirit properly, how to relate to fellow believers, how to be a healthy member of the Lord's church, how to execute their calling, and how to walk in honor. These are all subjects that equip the believer for success.

The rebellious become angered by the very concept of protocol. They will be shocked when they get to heaven. Angels are not just roaming around doing what they want; they are on an assignment led by the Lord of hosts! Everything in heaven has proper protocol, position, function, and rank. These principles must be understood on earth.

The apostle Paul went to great lengths to establish apostolic order in the burgeoning New Testament church.

> For this reason I left you in Crete, that you would set
> in order what remains and appoint elders in every city
> as I directed you.
>
> —TITUS 1:5, NASB

Paul left Titus as his ambassador to establish kingdom order. The Greek word for *order* in this verse means "to set in order besides or further," "put in order, correct," "to straighten further," and "to correct in addition."[5] Titus was being sent to examine what was being established, identify the weak points, and then properly correct and arrange it to align with kingdom purpose and protocol.

Ambassadors understand protocol. They know that they represent a government and must adhere to certain customs. They do not just operate in their own methodology or preferences. Order does not mean restriction. It should actually mean freedom but within the proper context of God's Word. Honorable people embrace order and instruction. They adhere to kingdom protocol.

Honorable people have good names! Their names are associated with their character. God's name is powerful because He is honorable. You can take Him at His Word. As we are continually being transformed into His image and likeness, we increase as our character is developed.

> The name of the LORD is a strong tower; the righteous
> run into it and are safe.
>
> —PROVERBS 18:10

The Lord's name is filled with protection! His name is honorable. Demons shake and tremble at the name of Jesus. In His name the sick are healed, and bondage is broken.

Therefore God highly exalted Him and gave Him the name which is above every name, that at the name of Jesus every knee should bow, of those in heaven and on earth and under the earth, and every tongue should confess that Jesus Christ is Lord, to the glory of God the Father.

—Philippians 2:9–11

We use the name of Jesus as a weapon against the enemy. We are to honor and lift up His name. We are *not* to misrepresent His name. Our lives should reflect the brilliance of His name.

Let love be genuine. Abhor what is evil; hold fast to what is good. Love one another with brotherly affection. Outdo one another in showing honor. Do not be slothful in zeal, be fervent in spirit, serve the Lord. Rejoice in hope, be patient in tribulation, be constant in prayer. Contribute to the needs of the saints and seek to show hospitality.

—Romans 12:9–13, esv

We are charged to honor one another. What would it look like if we showed honor to other believers? What would it look like if we honored people even when we don't agree with them on every point? Most people cannot do that because they connect honor with agreement, but honor is deeper than that.

Honorable people enjoy favor and celebrate others. Dishonorable people love to tear others down and watch them stumble. They rejoice in the calamity of others. Honorable people know how to place value on the life and achievement of others.

In the culture of honor we celebrate who a person is without stumbling over who they are not.[6]

—Bill Johnson

How can we create a culture of honor in our lives? A culture is a set of behaviors and beliefs that belong to a particular group of people. As I have traveled to various nations, I've had to familiarize myself with the cultures of specific places to work effectively with the people. A culture contains its own code of conduct and ethics. That code influences the behavior of people within the culture.

Kingdom culture should be filled with honor. We establish this culture by changing the way we think, speak, and live. We begin by seeking out the wisdom of the Father and applying it to our lives.

> Therefore the LORD, the God of Israel, declares: "I promised that your house and the house of your father should go in and out before me forever," but now the LORD declares: "Far be it from me, for those who honor me I will honor, and those who despise me shall be lightly esteemed."
>
> —1 SAMUEL 2:30, ESV

The Lord said that those who honor Him will be honored by Him in return. Honor unveils promotion and secures favor with God. Those who live honorably strive to keep the ways of the Lord. They honor God with their lives and their obedience. They lift His ways and His will above their own.

As the mystery of honor unfolds in our lives, our passion is directed toward the kingdom and God's way of doing things. More simply, we look to *please God*. The result of honor is promotion. Honorable people will be promoted because they are putting God first.

PROPHETIC PRAYER

Lord, I pray for the unveiling of the mystery of honor in my life. I decree that I walk in honor and integrity. I decree that I love Your ways and Your plans. I decree that I am an honorable person. Highlight any areas of dishonor in my life, and help me by the work of Your Spirit to bring those areas under subjection to You. I love You and Your kingdom. I love Your ways. I love Your plans. I love Your people, in the name of Jesus. Amen.

MY DECREE OVER YOU

I decree honor and glory are rising in your life. I decree radical and outrageous worship. I decree undignified adoration. I see the Father lavishing His love on you, and I see you responding as a lovesick child. I see you leaping into His arms with joy. I see your pathway marked by radical glory. I see revelation erupting from moments of glory. You were born for the honor and the glory.

POINTS TO CONSIDER

- What areas of my life need a deeper revelation of honor?
- Have I fully embraced the link between giving and honor?

- Do I have any remnants of religious thinking concerning generosity?
- Am I able to give generously to others? — yes
- Do I support vision when I connect and sow where I am blessed?
- Am I able to submit to and support key leaders in my life? —

① Honor with my tongue, with my patience and honor t'ward my husband.

② Giving - thank you for Your generous heart

③ Pray for Ted & Lori -
  · Reveal the mystery of honor
  · Decree honor + integrity in their lives
    ·.. and ours
  · Increased worship.
      ⌐ Bridges of worship
        · prayer
        · Kindness
  · Transformation in the next generation.

Increase my giving Lord to HONOR.

Chapter 3

THE MYSTERY
OF PROTECTION

I N THE JOCHEBED anointing God imparts supernatural protection. There is nothing like God's hand of protection upon your life. When God declares an unusual purpose over you, it should be no shock that the enemy shows up with unusual resistance. I always tell people to let spiritual warfare be a confirmation and not a discouragement. If you were not a threat to hell, the enemy would not be on the scene.

In the case of Jochebed and the birth of Moses, an evil ruler oppressed God's people. However, the spiritual principle, the law in the kingdom, is that seeds break cycles. Pharaoh feared the power of the seed of deliverance that God was about to bring forth, so he made a death decree.

> Joseph died, as did all his brothers, and all that generation. Nevertheless, the sons of Israel were fruitful, and increased abundantly, and multiplied, and became exceedingly mighty, so that the land was filled with them.
>
> Now there rose up a new king over Egypt, who did not know Joseph. He said to his people, "Surely, the people of the sons of Israel are more numerous and powerful than we. Come, let us deal wisely with them,

lest they multiply, and it come to pass that when any war breaks out, they also join our enemies, and fight against us, and escape from the land."

Therefore they set taskmasters over them to afflict them with their labor. They built for Pharaoh storage cities: Pithom and Rameses. But the more they afflicted them, the more they multiplied and grew so that as a result they abhorred the sons of Israel. The Egyptians made the children of Israel to serve with rigor, and they made their lives bitter with hard service—in mortar and in brick, and in all manner of service in the field, all their service in which they made them serve was with rigor.

The king of Egypt spoke to the Hebrew midwives, of which the name of one was Shiphrah, and the name of the other Puah, and he said, "When you perform the office of a midwife to the Hebrew women and see them on the stools, if it is a son, then you must kill him, but if it is a daughter, then she may live."

—EXODUS 1:6–16

The law of the land was death to all the male Hebrew children. The spirit of murder had been released upon the people. Any time there is wickedness and evil government, you will find the spirit of murder. The enemy hates God's people and wants to wipe them out! He plans to kill the seed. Despite the heinous activities of the enemy, God has unusual protection for His children.

Even in the midst of this plan of the enemy, God had a better plan. The Lord always has protection for His people. There may be a calamity or a crisis in the earth, but God has a plan. When fear enters, it will try to abort your faith, but the key is to stay in faith and stay in kingdom operation.

> And there went a man of the house of Levi, and took
> to wife a daughter of Levi. And the woman conceived,
> and bare a son: and when she saw him that he was a
> goodly child, she hid him three months.
>
> —Exodus 2:1–2, kjv

Moses' parents hid him at a time when he was supposed to be put to death. God was with them. They refused to bow to an evil edict. They were fearless in their pursuit of protection of their son! They would not allow the enemy to rob their seed.

While this is dealing with a natural seed, let's take a deeper look at what it implies in our own lives. What spiritual seeds planted in our lives has the enemy tried to assassinate? What plans and purposes are under siege right now? What prophetic words have you received that hell has come against? You can rest assured that evil forces will attempt to abort the launch God has for you. God has already ordained a higher realm of operation, and Satan is coming against it. He wants to knock it out before you even get going.

In the Jochebed anointing we find unusual protection. God covered this mother and her child! He hid them in the midst of the plans of destruction. Jochebed and Amram lived under the protection of the Lord. You experience the mystery of protection when you stay in the glory. When you disregard the curses and refuse to fight in the flesh, God's protection will show up in your life.

> For the Lord your God is He that goes with you, to
> fight for you against your enemies, to save you.
>
> —Deuteronomy 20:4

In this passage God is reminding Israel of His protection of them as a people. He had brought them out of Egyptian bondage and kept them safe in His glory. This promise still speaks to the people of God today. The Lord is fighting for us and with us. We do not have to be fearful. He is mighty, and our enemies will be defeated if we stay in His shadow! He affirms this in Psalm 91.

> He who dwells in the shelter of the Most High shall abide under the shadow of the Almighty. I will say of the LORD, "He is my refuge and my fortress, my God in whom I trust."
>
> Surely He shall deliver you from the snare of the hunter and from the deadly pestilence. He shall cover you with His feathers, and under His wings you shall find protection; His faithfulness shall be your shield and wall. You shall not be afraid of the terror by night, nor of the arrow that flies by day; nor of the pestilence that pursues in darkness, nor of the destruction that strikes at noonday. A thousand may fall at your side and ten thousand at your right hand, but it shall not come near you. Only with your eyes shall you behold and see the reward of the wicked.
>
> Because you have made the LORD, who is my refuge, even the Most High, your dwelling, there shall be no evil befall you, neither shall any plague come near your tent; for He shall give His angels charge over you to guard you in all your ways. They shall bear you up in their hands, lest you strike your foot against a stone. You shall tread upon the lion and adder; the young lion and the serpent you shall trample underfoot.
>
> Because he has set his love upon Me, therefore I will deliver him; I will set him on high, because he has known My name. He shall call upon Me, and I will answer him; I will be with him in trouble, and I will

deliver him and honor him. With long life I will satisfy him and show him My salvation.

These verses speak of dwelling (remaining and abiding) under the shadow of the Almighty. We find the mystery of protection in the place of "up-close living." To enjoy God's unusual protection, we need to be shadow dwellers. What is a shadow dweller?

One day as I was meditating upon this passage for most of that day, the Lord spoke to me about shadows and dwelling under His shadow. He asked me a question: "Ryan, how do you come under someone's shadow?" I pondered and then responded to the Lord. I told Him you have to be close to that person. He then spoke to me that this is the key to these verses, also one of the keys of divine protection. Shadow dwellers stay close. They are happiest in the presence of God and find their pleasure right beside Him.

> When she could no longer hide him, she took for him a container made of bulrushes and daubed it with tar and with pitch. She then put the child in it and set it in the reeds by the river's bank. Then his sister stood afar off so that she might know what would happen to him.
>
> The daughter of Pharaoh came down to wash herself at the river while her maidens walked along by the river's side, and when she saw the container among the reeds, she sent her maid, and she retrieved it. When she opened it, she saw the child. He was crying. She had compassion on him and said, "This is one of the Hebrews' children."
>
> —Exodus 2:3–6

After three months Jochebed could no longer hide her baby. God had protected their entire family, but now they needed another miracle. What was God's answer? He directed her to put her baby into a river commonly associated with Egyptian idol worship!

Imagine the faith that it would take to put your newborn into a river. Not just any river, but one where pagans worshipped false gods and performed demonic rituals. It would take unfathomable obedience and supernatural courage to do what she was about to do.

She made a floating basket and placed her baby in the water. God had a plan! Even when she had to release the seed, God's protection was there. Had she done according to her own thinking or wisdom, she would have missed it, but she was daring. She heard God and obeyed.

When the mystery of protection is unraveled in your life, other people won't understand your actions. They don't have to! You are not accountable to them. You are accountable for hearing and doing the word of the Lord. The word of the Lord releases His protection.

God had Pharaoh's daughter at the river at exactly the right time! God placed compassion in the house of Pharaoh for Moses, even though he was a Hebrew. The Egyptian ruler was determined to kill Hebrew boys, but God said no! God moves in the opposite direction of evil decrees or wicked systems in the lives of His people. This story of protection so wild, so outrageous, and so supernatural will set people free!

God protects His people through revelation. He uses the prophetic anointing to reveal, to warn, to discern, and to know. I am not just talking about prophets. Prophets are a part of the plan, but so are prophetic believers. Those who hear, see, and know are vital pieces in God's big, beautiful puzzle.

One Hebrew word associated with prophets and prophetic ministry is *shamar*. *Shamar* means to keep, watch, and preserve. We need shamar prophets, prophetic teams, and prophetic ministry. We need clear and concise words of the Lord. The word of the Lord literally arms us for battle.

In private and corporate prayer shamar words are vital. God will warn His people of demonic plans before they manifest in the earth realm. When God issues the warning, there is a call to ascend and pray. These things are defeated in the realm of the spirit. We cannot overcome what we do not discern.

I remember a time when I received a powerful shamar word from another leader. I had traveled with a prophetic friend of mine to another nation. My friend was preaching a morning session when he stopped right in the middle to prophesy over me. He declared a sifting was coming to my inner circle, but that it was God and He would protect and guide me. I had also received this same word during a time of private prayer. God was arming me for the coming battle.

It unfolded just as the Lord had said! There was both sifting and shaking. It was turbulent and uncomfortable, but God had a plan! I had numerous people come to me concerned and afraid that the enemy was doing all of it, but I confidently told them that it was the hand of the Lord. You see, I had already been to the future through the word of the Lord! The shamar word of the Lord takes you into the future.

In *The Prophet's Manual* John Eckhardt writes:

> Additionally, the word *shamar* identifies a prophet who encircles (or surrounds) to retain and attend to, as one does a garden. The prophet's spiritual authority acts as a fence or garrison around an assigned congregation to shield it from harm, attack, or demonic trespass. Protection from trespassers, as meant here, includes protection from the spoilage, destruction, invasion, and threats that result from spiritual and human trespassers in the church.

> Behold, he that keepeth [*shamar*] Israel
> shall neither slumber nor sleep. The
> LORD is thy keeper [*shamar*]: the LORD
> is thy shade upon thy right hand. The
> sun shall not smite thee by day, nor the
> moon by night. The LORD shall preserve
> [*shamar*] thee from all evil: he shall pre-
> serve [*shamar*] thy soul. The LORD shall
> preserve [*shamar*] thy going out and thy
> coming in from this time forth, and even
> for evermore.
> —PSALM 121:4–8 [KJV]

We can see from these verses that God shamars His
people. God loves His people and protects them. The
shamar aspect of the prophet's ministry is a part of the
nature of God. God never slumbers or sleeps. He is
always alert. God shamars us from evil. God shamars
our souls (our minds, wills, and emotions). God
shamars our going out and coming in (our travels). It is
the nature of God to protect. Protection from God is a
part of our covenant with Him, and shamar prophets
are therefore a practical part of the working out of our
covenant relationship with God.[1]

Watchmen wait for the word of the Lord. They stand at
attention, listening and looking to see what God would say.

> My soul waits for the Lord, more than watchmen for
> the morning, more than watchmen for the morning.
> —PSALM 130:6

We must incorporate active listening into our spiritual lives.
We must be quick to hear and heed the warning of the Lord,

both individually and corporately, as this is one of the functions of the prophetic anointing when it is properly stewarded and matured.

OPEN EYES AND OPEN EARS

One of God's warning systems in our lives is the gift of discerning of spirits.

> ...to another the working of miracles, to another prophecy, to another discerning of spirits, to another various kinds of tongues, and to another the interpretation of tongues.
>
> —1 CORINTHIANS 12:10

In this verse the apostle Paul is listing the gifts of the Spirit. I call them God's power tools. One of these gifts is the discerning of spirits. It is the divine ability to see and know which spirit is motivating a person or situation. When the discerning of spirits is in operation, it is like pulling the curtain back to reveal what is behind. This is an innately prophetic concept. The prophetic anointing continually pulls back the veil and shines light on things.

> ...and after the earthquake a fire; but the LORD was not in the fire: and after the fire a still small voice.
>
> —1 KINGS 19:12, KJV

The Lord revealed Himself to Elijah in the still small voice! This was an old covenant prophet. This was not a new covenant believer with the Holy Spirit on the inside and a born-again human spirit. We are hardwired to hear from God. We have spiritual senses that ping and give off distress signals. Our spiritual senses are complex! We have eyes in the spirit realm!

The voice of the Lord can speak to you whether in a whisper, as in the still small voice; a thundering voice; or the audible voice of God. You can also receive subtle communication as God releases instructions spoken to your inner man. This flows like an inner conversation. You hear the direction of the Lord released to you as a voice on the inside of you.

Your spiritual ears have been formed to receive the spoken word of the Lord. You need to decree ears that hear! You need to declare fresh revelation in your life. You need to make intentional listening a part of your regular routine.

> Behold, I stand at the door, and knock: if any man hear my voice, and open the door, I will come in to him, and will sup with him, and he with me. To him that overcometh will I grant to sit with me in my throne, even as I also overcame, and am set down with my Father in his throne. He that hath an ear, let him hear what the Spirit saith unto the churches.
> —REVELATION 3:20–22, KJV

You also have spiritual eyes. The apostle Paul prayed for the opening of his spiritual eyes. What do eyes do? They see! Spiritual eyes receive pictures, visions, dreams, and visual leading. The Spirit of God can lead you by what you see. This is critical in the discerning of spirits.

> …that the God of our Lord Jesus Christ, the Father of glory, may give unto you the spirit of wisdom and revelation in the knowledge of him: the eyes of your understanding being enlightened; that ye may know what is the hope of his calling, and what the riches of the glory of his inheritance in the saints.
> —EPHESIANS 1:17–18, KJV

Some of my most profound assignments have come through prophetic dreams from the Lord. They have shifted my life, sent me warnings, and shown me who to connect with and who to disconnect from. I have learned to pray and pay attention to the dream realm. It is one of the most powerful ways God speaks to me. It has literally rescued me time and again! I thank God for spiritual eyes that see!

God can provide alerts through our spiritual eyes and ears. The gift of discerning of spirits operates by the Spirit of the Lord to help us know which spirit is motivating a person or situation. This gift uses our spiritual senses to reveal this truth to us. Many believers miss these kinds of warnings because they have not developed a strong understanding of spiritual senses.

You can receive impressions, thoughts, and subtle revelations by the mind of the Spirit.

> And he that searcheth the hearts knoweth what is the mind of the Spirit, because he maketh intercession for the saints according to the will of God.
> —Romans 8:27, kjv

When you receive warnings from the mind of the Spirit, they can come in a variety of ways.

+ **God thoughts**. These are illuminations that come like thoughts but are born of the Spirit.

+ **Impressions.** These are almost like feelings, yet they're not mental but spiritual. You have an impression about something or someone that is deeper than a thought.

+ **Inward knowing.** This is when you just know something by the Spirit, and there is no escaping it. It did not come to you through a tremendous encounter but just a simple knowing.

+ **Leading.** This is a prompting or guiding to move in a particular direction in a matter.

+ **Prompting.** This is an unction that you cannot escape. You feel directed to do something.

You have other spiritual senses just like your natural man. For instance, you can have a spiritual sense of taste! You can begin to taste something that indicates a spiritual atmosphere or climate. As it pertains to a motive, when you are around a person and you receive a foul taste, this is indicating something demonic. Demons look ugly, they smell ugly, and they can present a disgusting taste in your mouth.

> How sweet are your words to my taste, sweeter than honey to my mouth!
>
> —Psalm 119:103, niv

> As newborn babies, desire the pure milk of the word, that by it you may grow, if it is true that you have experienced that the Lord is good.
>
> —1 Peter 2:2–3

Another powerful spiritual sense is the sense of smell! Sometimes discernment will operate through smell. You can smell the fragrance of heaven, and often you can smell the presence of a demon. I have ministered to or come in contact with persons in need of deliverance who had an unclean, foul smell.

> I will accept you with your sweet savour, when I bring you out from the people, and gather you out of the

countries wherein ye have been scattered; and I will be
sanctified in you before the heathen.

—EZEKIEL 20:41, KJV

And walk in love, as Christ also hath loved us, and
hath given himself for us an offering and a sacrifice to
God for a sweet smelling savour.

—EPHESIANS 5:2, KJV

But I have all, and abound: I am full, having received
of Epaphroditus the things which were sent from
you, an odour of a sweet smell, a sacrifice acceptable,
wellpleasing to God.

—PHILIPPIANS 4:18, KJV

An important aspect of discerning spirits is not to overlook a
check in your spirit. A check is a warning in your inner man. It
is the impression that something is not right. When you have
a check in your spirit, or you experience something that I have
described from your spiritual senses, do not just override it!
Pause, pay attention, and begin to pray. Not only can prayer
save your life, but all prophetic operations also require prayer
to administrate properly. You must pursue the full revelation.
Do not just stop because you don't have the full picture. Keep
pursuing.

The Bible tells us that people perish for lack of knowledge.
Many believers operate in a one-dimensional prophetic realm
when God wants to bring us into 4-D prophetic encounters. He
can reveal things to us in a variety of ways. This small section of
examples barely scratches the surface. To more fully understand
the prophetic realm, you need to study it and be activated in it.

God's kingdom also employs angels to protect His people.
Angels are assigned to us. They provide supernatural protection.
In Psalm 91:11 God tells us that He will give His angels

instructions to protect us! We have heavenly backup and supernatural warriors on our side.

> See that you do not despise one of these little ones, for
> I say to you that their angels in heaven continually see
> the face of My Father who is in heaven.
> —MATTHEW 18:10, NASB

I love this verse! God is revealing His value for each of His children. He assigns angels to protect us against the plans of hell. God has angels on assignment with direct access to Him, bringing vital communication from heaven to earth. Angels are active and working to see kingdom plans come to pass. We do not need to be afraid of the angelic host but need to embrace their ministry in our lives and in the kingdom of God.

> For it is written: "He will command His angels
> concerning you to guard you carefully."
> —LUKE 4:10, NIV

Satan was tempting Jesus. He challenged Jesus to throw Himself off the highest point of the temple. He cited that God would protect Jesus with His angels. Satan was twisting Psalm 91. The devil knows the Word. He knows how to twist it and omit key points to deceive even the very elect if possible. This is exactly what he was doing in this instance. He was intentionally leaving out the portion that says, "in all your ways." The reality is that God sends angelic protection to those who are committed to His loving care, not to those who want to put Him to a false test.

> See, I am sending an angel ahead of you to guard you along the way and to bring you to the place I have prepared.
> —Exodus 23:20, NIV

God used a mighty angel in the protection of Israel as they journeyed into the Promised Land. The angel was charged with their guidance and well-being. Angels are assigned to protect the people of God and make sure we get to where He is taking us! Angels are a part of God's plans of protection in our lives. They are supernatural warriors working with us and for us because we are the heirs of salvation.

The blood of Jesus is another part of our protection package. In Exodus the presence of the blood caused death to pass over the homes of the Hebrews. This was a type and shadow of the blood of the spotless Lamb that would come to eradicate the sins of the world. The blood of Jesus has defeated and conquered the power of death, hell, and the grave! Because of the power of the blood of Jesus, you can come boldly into the presence of God. The blood of Jesus builds a mighty wall between sin and believers who have been made the righteousness of God through Jesus (2 Cor. 5:21).

Anytime God leads you into an assignment, there is divine protection. It is critical to walk by faith and claim the protection of the Lord. Through prophetic insight there is protection. Through His Word there is protection. The Lord will send the right leaders and ministry gifts to speak into your life and issue warnings, instruction, and keys for your protection. Pay extra attention to the voices that you are connected to. Through His anointing there is protection! The anointing will shatter and destroy the powers of hell. Protection is intricately linked with the plan of God for your life.

PROPHETIC PRAYER

Lord, I thank You for divine protection in my life. I thank You that no weapon formed against me prospers. I thank You for the angels of the Lord protecting me. I thank You for Your glory covering me. I decree that I am supernaturally safeguarded, in the name of Jesus. Amen.

MY DECREE OVER YOU

I decree unusual and supernatural protection over your life. I decree your steps are ordained and ordered by the Father. I see Him guiding you into new territory and releasing the angelic hosts to protect you. I see you moving in tremendous purpose and destiny. As you are supernaturally led, directed, and elevated, you are also shielded from every plan of the enemy.

POINTS TO CONSIDER

- For every plan there is protection.
- The blood of Jesus provides a shield.
- Have you claimed, activated, and understood the discerning of spirits?

- ᕽ What examples in your life are there of God speaking to you and you overriding His warning?

- ᕽ Are you quick to listen to His warning?

- ᕽ The angels of the Lord are a surrounding force.

- ᕽ You can agree with the Word of God and release angelic protection.

- ᕽ The name of the Lord is a strong tower!

- ᕽ Use the name of Jesus as a protective weapon against the enemy.

- ᕽ God can cause your enemy to pass by!

- ᕽ He can hide you from the adversary.

Chapter 4

THE MYSTERY OF TIMING

G OD'S TIMING IS one of the most remarkable elements in the lives of Jochebed and Moses. There is a mystery in the principle of divine timing. Heaven has arranged breathtaking plans and exploits for your life, but seasons and rhythms must be understood and pursued. The following verse in Ecclesiastes is one of the most familiar passages concerning timing. Every purpose has an assigned time!

> There is a time for everything, and a season for every
> activity under the heavens.
> —ECCLESIASTES 3:1, NIV

Missing God's timing concerning destiny can be a critical mistake. In the journey of Jochebed there was supernatural timing in every step. As you press into the glory of God to pursue His plans for your life, family, and purpose in the earth, you must accurately discern the time. No purpose is created without the assignment of moments and seasons. There are moments to wait, to observe, to launch, and to build.

A submitted life is one that waits patiently on the Lord. This is one of the most remarkable acts of trust and obedience, just to sit when your mind is ready to launch forward and your spirit is filled with revelation. There is a simplicity and a depth in the waiting. I laugh when people tell me it seems as if I sprang up from nowhere; they don't understand my long season of waiting on the Lord and seeking His perfect plan.

Anyone can jump forward because they feel stirred! It is easy to have a sense of destiny and want to take action. It takes prayer, labor, and pursuit of the Father's heart to wait. Yet the waiting is beautiful!

> I waited patiently for the LORD, and He turned to me, and heard my cry.
> —PSALM 40:1

> He has made everything beautiful in its appropriate time. He has also put obscurity in their hearts so that no one comes to know the work that God has done from the beginning to the end.
> —ECCLESIASTES 3:11

God has already mapped out the beginning and the end. He has a plan for both the highs and the lows. You may not feel or be aware of it, but if you have surrendered your life to Him, He is working even now. His plans are alive and active even in the moments when the waiting becomes difficult. He makes all things beautiful in His timing. In the waiting there are deep and meaningful lessons to learn, giants to confront, and mantles to catch.

THE GIFT OF THE WAIT

One of God's gifts to you is called the wait. At the time it may seem more like a burden than a gift. What is the wait? It is that time after a thing has been revealed when you are required to be patient until it has come to pass.

> "The LORD is my portion," says my soul, "therefore I
> will hope in Him." The LORD is good to those who
> wait for Him, to the soul who seeks Him.
> —LAMENTATIONS 3:24–25

It's reckless to step into an assignment before God has adequately prepared you. Most of the time we are quick to step out because of our immaturity. In the wait God leads us back to the cross, and we lay down wrong motives, impure ambition, and false concepts. The wait is the place to perfect our character. Mistaking gifts and spiritual abilities for maturity is easy. I have seen it many, many times. Someone can prophesy strongly, sing well, or preach powerfully, but integrity is lacking and his or her life is a wreck. The ability that the person carries is a gift. Gifts are supported by character, and character is developed over time. There is a process of character development that is not always easy, but it is imperative to fulfill purpose.

Mature believers are not intimidated or frustrated by waiting. They have submitted to God's process, willingly laid it all down, and prepared their hearts to seek the Father. They are cooperating with the plan of preparation. I find no place in the Word of God where a man or woman was sent without a process. They were first prepared for the journey, and when the time was right, they went. David spent time alone learning to worship and to war. He killed the lion and the bear before the time came for him to be raised up to confront a giant.

> David said to Saul, "Your servant was a shepherd for
> my father's flock, and the lion came and the bear, and
> took a lamb out of the flock. And I went out after him,
> and struck him, and delivered it out of his mouth. And
> when he arose against me, I took hold of his beard,
> struck him, and killed him. Your servant slew both the

lion and the bear. And this uncircumcised Philistine will be as one of them, because he has reviled the armies of the living God." David said, "The LORD who delivered me out of the paw of the lion and out of the paw of the bear, He will deliver me out of the hand of this Philistine."

—1 Samuel 17:34–37

David was sent into the field as a simple shepherd while his brothers were at battle. He was excluded from the activities of his family. Even when the prophet came to his house to anoint a new king, his own father rejected him and left him out. God was the One who called him in and anointed him in the midst of those who rejected him!

What if David had rushed the process? What if he became wounded and bitter because of the actions of his father and brothers, and he just gave up? What kept his heart pure? Worship!

LORD, how my foes have multiplied! Many rise up against me! Many are saying about my life, "There is no help for him in God." Selah

But You, O LORD, are a shield for me, my glory and the One who raises up my head. I cried to the LORD with my voice, and He answered me from His holy hill. Selah

—Psalm 3:1–4

These words were written in one of the darkest times of the life of David. He was enduring the bitter betrayal of his son Absalom. In the midst of that dark period David employed the weaponry that lifted him from the shepherd's field and into the palace. He worshipped God! The presence of God kept David from journeying down the dark road of anger and rejection. He kept coming back to Yahweh over and over.

The presence of God will keep you, refine you, and cleanse you! There is nothing else like the presence of God. Once you have tasted of His power and majesty, you will forever be ruined to normality and complacency. You will have a deep desire for God's presence, His glory.

As David was tending the sheep, he encountered the lions and the bears. He faced ravenous animals and defeated them. He would never have encountered them if he was not in an isolated place. That experience prepared him to defeat Goliath.

In the darkest times of the wait there is still purpose! This is the mystery of the wait. When you cannot feel or see the hands of the Father, they are still there and moving on your behalf. The enemy is masterful at creating a false narrative. He has been lying to humanity and twisting things since the beginning of creation. He knows how to speak to men and women in a way that woos their emotions.

The wait will reveal your impatience. The wait will reveal your insecurities. When you have been told no, your heart will be tested. When a door is closed that you really believed you were going to walk through, you will be tested. What will you do? Will you fold it up and quit? Will you run back to old bondage? Will you seek shelter in wrong places and fleshly comforts?

These things are revealed in the wait. The heart is tried in the wait. When David was brought to the front lines of the battle, he pointed back to the obstacles and challenges of the wait. He knew that he had confidence in God because of where he had already been.

God's purpose is to prepare your heart and qualify you in the wait. He wants to cut certain things off and bring you into greater trust and dependency upon His grace, to ignite your faith and release hope, and to invite you into portions of His faithfulness as you wait.

> In those days, when Moses was grown, he went out to his brothers and looked on their burdens; and he saw an Egyptian striking a Hebrew, one of his brothers. He looked this way and that way, and when he saw no one, he killed the Egyptian and hid him in the sand. When he went out the next day, two men of the Hebrews struggled with each other; and he said to him that did the wrong, "Why do you strike your companion?"
>
> He said, "Who made you a prince and a judge over us? Do you intend to kill me as you killed the Egyptian?" Moses feared and said, "Surely this thing is known."
>
> Now when Pharaoh heard this thing, he sought to slay Moses. But Moses fled from the presence of Pharaoh and settled in the land of Midian, and he dwelled by a well.
>
> —Exodus 2:11–15

Moses was called to be a deliverer. He was established as God's answer to injustice. One of the dimensions of the Jochebed anointing is the glory to birth deliverers and deliverance. Moses understood his life's mission, but he stepped out prematurely.

This action demands an answer to a deeper question, why do we step into something we are truly not ready for? There can be several answers, but one of the most fundamental is immaturity. We are simply stirred in our emotions and refuse to allow the process to prepare us adequately.

Over my years in ministry I have seen many people fall into this dangerous pattern. A person gets a glimpse of his calling and responds with little to no wisdom. Then when God sends seasoned voices to warn him, he lashes out in anger and rebellion. This is immaturity and carnality. This type of fleshly response demonstrates a lack of authentic wisdom.

> Who among you is wise and intelligent? Let him by his good conduct show his [good] deeds with the gentleness and humility of true wisdom. But if you have bitter jealousy and selfish ambition in your hearts, do not be arrogant, and [as a result] be in defiance of the truth.
>
> This [superficial] wisdom is not that which comes down from above, but is earthly (secular), natural (unspiritual), even demonic. For where jealousy and selfish ambition exist, there is disorder [unrest, rebellion] and every evil thing and morally degrading practice.
>
> But the wisdom from above is first pure [morally and spiritually undefiled], then peace-loving [courteous, considerate], gentle, reasonable [and willing to listen], full of compassion and good fruits. It is unwavering, without [self-righteous] hypocrisy [and self-serving guile].
>
> —JAMES 3:13–17, AMP

Many people fall into the trap of self-serving and carnal wisdom that feeds their egos. This is dangerous in the pursuit of a spiritual calling as it leads to self-gratification and not service to God's people. Carnal wisdom might verify something that heaven has not yet approved. Many believers become more rooted in fleshly advice and ambition than in scriptural principles and God's process for their lives.

Failing to recognize that your calling will demand an intense process of preparation is dangerous. God cannot trust you with the minds and hearts of His family until your mind and heart become fully surrendered and cleansed. This is the purpose of the process.

When Moses stepped forward, someone died! There is a warning here. When we step into a purpose before we are ready, there will be casualties. I recall an excellent example of this. Some years ago I advised a young couple to wait on a church plant and not jump into it at that moment. I gave them several concerns. All they heard was that I was holding them back. They ignored my advice, stepped out, and made the exact mistakes that I had tried to forewarn them about. The end result was that the young church folded and there was much hurt all the way around. I wonder how many casualties we have had in the kingdom because ambition spoke louder than wisdom.

Moses retreated and spent an intense season running from the call. He was discouraged. We would call it spiritual warfare, but in reality it was the result of improper timing. Launching out into something before we are prepared sets us up for unnecessary hurts and discouragement. The loving heart of the Father provides guidance, assurance, and right timing.

> Love is patient, love is kind and is not jealous; love does not brag and is not arrogant.
> —1 CORINTHIANS 13:4, NASB

Within the boundaries of love there is a willingness to be patient, a willingness to wait. Through love we can come to a healthy place of effectively waiting upon the Lord.

Webster's defines *arrogant* as "exaggerating or disposed to exaggerate one's own worth or importance often by an overbearing manner [as in] an *arrogant* official; showing an offensive attitude of superiority: proceeding from or characterized by arrogance."[1]

Love is not arrogant. It is not overbearing or self-promoting. Those who refuse to wait often deem their own gifts and voices as superior. They do not value the wisdom and leadership of others. This is dangerous and opens the doorway for a spirit of deception to enter.

A true gift from God must be consecrated. It must be set apart and purified so that God, not man, will get all the glory. Anytime we are pursuing our own superiority above the faithfulness of the cross, we are in error. For this reason consistent prayer and time in the presence of God is vital. God's sweet and intimate presence will purify the heart and place a blazing fire of purification upon a gift.

> The end of a matter is better than the beginning of it,
> and the patient in spirit than the haughty in spirit.
> —Ecclesiastes 7:8

PROPHETIC PRAYER

Father, I thank You for the gift of waiting. I value Your timing and long to be in sync with You. I decree that I walk in divine timing in my life. I follow Your voice, but the voice of a stranger I do not hear. I bind up impatience and frustration. I will not allow my flesh to mislead me. I confess that I am patient and kind, and I am not arrogant. I confess that I am submitted to Your timing, Lord. I thank You, Father, for divine guidance and rhythm in my life, in the name of Jesus. Amen.

MY DECREE OVER YOU

I decree perfect timing and planning in your life. I decree the proper process of development for your destiny. I see you moving in God's timing and grace. I see it all coming together for you. The enemy said it would not work, but he is a liar. I see the loving hands of the Father arranging every assignment, relationship, and mandate in your life. He is leading you through the process. You will see, hear, and know His will for you in every area, in Jesus' name. Amen.

POINTS TO CONSIDER

- In what areas have I failed?
- Have I failed because I stepped out too swiftly?
- Do I see pride manifesting in the areas of my calling and assignment?
- Have other people been hurt because of my failure to wait?

If the answer is yes to any of the above, do not take on condemnation but choose to move ahead in wisdom and God's timing. Commit to pray more fervently for right timing in your life.

- Am I able to see beauty in the waiting in my life?
- Am I able to see the hand of God at work in delays?
- Am I trusting deeply enough?

Chapter 5

THE MYSTERY
OF THE LAUNCH

IN STUDYING THE unique mysteries of the Jochebed anointing and the story of her son Moses, we cannot overlook the mystery of the launch! There is an appointed time when the force of heaven accelerates your destiny with a sudden burst of forward motion. I call this the launch! This is a mystery to many because they work to manufacture their own launches.

While I certainly understand the gift of free will, the power of our choices, and the impact of sowing, I also believe God holds the launch codes for our destiny! You and I are not orphans left to fend for ourselves. When temptation arises to manufacture something that heaven has not orchestrated, we are moving in the mentality and spirit of an orphan. It is our own impatience and insecurity with the voice of the enemy colliding to get us in the flesh.

> For the one who sows to his own flesh will from the flesh reap corruption, but the one who sows to the Spirit will from the Spirit reap eternal life.
> —GALATIANS 6:8

The enemy will attempt to trap you in broken patterns of sowing into the fleshly realm, not the spirit realm. This is a tactic aimed to produce a corrupt harvest. When you attempt to launch yourself, you run the risk of reaping corruption. This is not to say that you should be lazy or not work diligently to partner with the prophetic words and mandate over your life. It simply means you cannot afford to act as an orphan—self-guiding, self-protecting, and self-providing. This is a demonic trap that aborts the rights and privileges of sonship.

We get a better understanding of a corrupt harvest by breaking down the word *corruption* in Galatians 6:8. The Greek word *phthora* translated as corruption in this verse means "destruction, corruption." It can mean "destruction from internal corruption (deterioration, decay); rottenness, perishableness, corruption, decay, decomposition."[1] When people build their lives on carnal thinking, set their own boundaries, and sow continually into the realm of the flesh, the end result is a bankrupt, temporal harvest filled with depravity.

According to Webster's, the word *launch* means "to throw forward: hurl; to release, catapult, or send off (a self-propelled object); to set (a boat or ship) afloat…to get off to a good start; to spring forward…to enter energetically…to make a start."[2]

As you ponder this definition, a clear prophetic picture emerges. God has an appointed time and mechanism to catapult, hurl, and release His people. He first declares their destiny, they hear, see, and know it, and then they accept it. He anoints them, they enter a process of preparation initiated by heaven, and suddenly a launch comes.

I believe right at this moment there are people, ministries, plans, and purposes on the launchpad. God has postponed them for a supernatural takeoff. He has initiated greatness inside each of His kids, but we must recognize this mystery of the launch.

What causes one to launch while another waits? We must believe in and discern God's timing. He will launch one while preparing another. We can get frustrated when someone else seems to be passing us, but the kingdom has perfect timing and plans. The enemy will try to trap our minds into making false comparisons. Though one person's destiny may be similar to that of another, it is still unique. We cannot afford to become envious of the launch of another. It will abort our launch and stall out the engines of our destiny.

> A sound heart is the life of the flesh, but envy the rottenness of the bones.
>
> —PROVERBS 14:30

Envy is rotten! It brings contamination to your life. You cannot afford to get mad that someone else is being afforded opportunity while you are waiting. You need to celebrate their launch and let it inspire you to believe that yours is coming.

I dealt with a tragic situation when jealousy manifested and turned demonic between two people who had similar ministries. One of them studied for a brief period under the ministry of a more seasoned minister when a sudden launch took place. The favor that manifested was absolutely supernatural and eruptive. This rising voice was promoted over and over again while stewarding a humble attitude and a genuine love for God and His people. It was beautiful to watch.

The other minister had stalled out and faced significant personal challenges. It seemed as though the rapid launch of the protégé was unfair. The older minister began to take a series of demonic steps to abort the launch of the other. It was a Cain and Abel type of situation. God kept promoting the upcoming leader while diminishing the influence of the accuser. This is what happens when wicked ambition, control, and bitterness take over. It will create a toxic portal for spirits of manipulation and witchcraft to enter.

God launches *whom* He chooses *when* He chooses and *how* He chooses. We can certainly observe scriptural principles, but He alone does it! This is the mystery of the launch. Our job is never to dictate how and who.

LISTEN FOR HIS COMMAND

> When He had finished speaking, He said to Simon, "Launch out into the deep and let down your nets for a catch."
>
> —LUKE 5:4

Jesus was challenging the mind of a skilled fisherman. Simon had toiled all night to no avail. His mind and body were tired, but the Lord asked him to launch out into the deep. He was issuing a dare. Launch out into the deep! Go into the unknown! Go out where it doesn't make any sense! Override your natural mind!

In my experience this is always the place where the mightiest miracles take place. You cannot stay in the safe zone and the miracle zone at the same time. They are two entirely different places. God challenges His people to launch into new ideas, new endeavors, new plans, and new prophetic concepts.

Many people miss their net-breaking harvest because they will not launch out when heaven declares it. Heaven was commissioning Simon Peter to go out and get a net-breaking harvest. He had to overcome his natural mindset and limitations. He had to trust in the power of God. He finally decided to obey Jesus and launch out. This is when the overwhelming breakthrough and harvest is realized. We must listen to His command and go despite our natural wisdom. When God speaks, power is loosed.

One of the vital elements in a launch is the word of the Lord.

I have never experienced a personal launch without prophetic guidance. The voice of the Lord provides a crucial road map and inspires faith in our hearts.

Prophetic atmospheres prepare you for the launch. You need to be in places where God's voice is honored and welcomed. People look for answers in empty places. Get in a church where the prophetic is embraced. Make friends with prophetic people. Listen to prophetic voices and create a prophetic atmosphere in your own home.

I remember a time a few years ago when God was speaking to my wife, Joy, and me about a new launch in our lives. We had received countless prophetic words about a transition and shift, but we seemed stuck. During that time the tender voice of the Lord gently nudged my heart to spend a specific time of the day in prayer. It was a clear leading to pray at a different time of day than I like to pray. I asked Father for grace. It became the most natural thing I had done. I found myself looking forward to those times with God.

As I was praying, God gave me many revelations and words for me and His people. Entire books came out of this time with God. Revivals were birthed. Tremendous, miraculous break-throughs came forth in my life and my ministry as a result of what God spoke to me during these times.

With God's help I created a prophetic atmosphere in my home and ministry. The word of the Lord was rich and the direction became clear. God brought about a sudden catapult and accelerated everything we were doing. As heaven spoke, the launch codes were supplied! Listen to prophets, prophetic words, and Spirit leadings; value the voice of the Lord.

FIVE STEPS FOR YOUR LAUNCH

1. Do a system check: make sure things are in order.

Alignment with heavenly plans and purposes prepares the launch. Check your connections and plans as a vital first step in the process of the launch.

> For who among you, intending to build a tower, does not sit down first and count the cost to see whether he has resources to complete it? Otherwise, perhaps, after he has laid the foundation and is not able to complete it, all who see it will begin to mock him, saying, "This man began to build and was not able to complete it."
>
> —LUKE 14:28–30

2. Do a safety check: make sure the gates are secured.

Make sure the perimeter is secured as you kick out the enemy and his lies. Fortify your thoughts and renew your mind. Do some spiritual warfare and kick Satan out of your life. You do not want to launch only to crash and burn! You want to soar on the winds of the Spirit. Let God cleanse your life.

> In that day this song shall be sung in the land of Judah: We have a strong city; He appoints walls and bulwarks for security. Open the gates, that the righteous nation may enter, the one who remains faithful.
>
> —ISAIAH 26:1–2

3. Wait for clearance.

This is critical. There is divine timing. God will make it plain for you. Do not get in a hurry! Do not allow fleshly ambition to create an unnecessary urge to jump when you are not ready. The Father knows what you can handle and when you are to go. Trust God.

> Surely the righteous man shall not be moved; the righteous shall be in everlasting remembrance. He shall not be afraid of evil tidings; his heart is fixed, trusting in the LORD.
>
> —PSALM 112:6–7

4. Begin the countdown!

There is a *kairos* timing and a prophetic countdown as you enter the final moments before you launch. When purpose is discovered, timing must be revealed. This only comes from the wisdom of the Lord. Don't move in zeal, but instead walk in wisdom and obedience.

> And let us not grow weary in doing good, for in due season we shall reap, if we do not give up.
>
> —GALATIANS 6:9

5. Don't abort the mission!

Disobedience and unbelief can abort the mission. You need radical, robust faith to launch effectively. Spend time building faith for your assignment. Do not let the voice of the enemy distract you or get you off course. Be quick to recognize his lies and cast them down.

> He did not waver at the promise of God through unbelief, but was strong in faith, giving glory to God.
>
> —ROMANS 4:20

When God's launch manifests, it is the time of sudden and rapid advance. You need to believe for launch! Decree the launch and lean in for prophetic understanding concerning your launch. It may seem impossible today, but I can assure you that when God is ready, you will launch boldly and rapidly into the destiny God has ordained for you!

LISTEN TO THE RIGHT VOICE

The right friends are critical during a launch. You can't go into the expanded place while you are listening to limited voices. God will stretch your relationships as He is preparing you for launch. Divine relationships will unfold during the season of your launch. The launch will cause some to stall out and try to hold you back. It is a hard truth, but you must realize that some people like the small version of you. They like the struggling version of you. When the promoted version shows up, they will become uncomfortable.

Some cannot go with you! Many times, when you move to another level, some choose not to go. Understand that it is a choice. God loves and has a plan for them, but they must yield. They must be willing to grow. You may be released from some small thinkers, some complainers, and some critics during your launch. You must learn whom to listen to and whom to ignore.

When David wanted to confront Goliath, his own brothers came against him.

> Eliab his eldest brother heard when he spoke to the men. And Eliab's anger was kindled against David, and he said, "Why have you come down here? And with whom have you left those few sheep in the wilderness? I know your pride and the evil of your heart. For you have come down that you might see the battle."
> —1 SAMUEL 17:28

David had a choice to make. Would he allow the negative thoughts and words of his brother to keep him from God's plan? It is a sad truth, but many human beings are simply not strong enough emotionally or spiritually to move ahead in the plan of God when their close friends or family members have critical things to say. They fear men more than God.

David ignored the words of his angry brother and followed God's plan instead. He took down the giant and received a significant promotion—all because of his obedience. Just like David, your obedience and radical boldness will empower *much* in your life. You must be intentional in the relationships in your life. You must not allow the words of the angry and those filled with unbelief to stop you. If God said it, then it is so! Your job is to believe, obey, and cooperate.

How do you handle those who cannot embrace your next season? Give them to God! You do not have ownership of them. They belong to the Father, and He has good plans for them. Release them, and let the Lord deal with them. Try to do so peacefully. Don't allow condemnation and works to hinder you. The enemy will try to condemn you. He uses that strategy to lock you in a toxic situation and abort your next level. Do not partner with it. People will feel guilty because a relationship changes seasons or courses. Have grace with people who simply cannot go with you. Pray for them and ask for the Father's love to surround them.

PROPHETIC PRAYER

Father, I thank You that right now You are preparing me for a sudden catapult. I believe that all promotion comes from You. I rest in Your grace. I thank You that You are ordaining the season of my life and You alone hold the keys to my promotion. I submit to Your timing and Your guidance. Give me the wisdom to successfully navigate each season and to observe the lessons You have taught so that I am prepared for my next level. I thank You for prophetic words and insight about my assignment. I thank You for ideas, strategies, and language for where You are taking me. I thank You for rapid and sudden favor and promotion, in the name of Jesus. Amen.

MY DECREE OVER YOU

I decree wise strategy in your life. I decree sudden and eruptive promotion and favor for your life. I command the right doors to open and the wrong ones to close. I break the power of guilt and condemnation in relationships, and I speak wisdom and grace in those areas of your life. I decree that you will rightly discern your destiny partners in each season. I decree that you will celebrate the launch of others and patiently wait upon your launch, in Jesus' name. Amen.

POINTS TO CONSIDER

- What is God speaking to you about the next season?
- What lessons are being provided right now?
- Are you able to rejoice when others are launched?
- Who in your life is excited about your promotion?
- Who in your life likes you to stay small?

- What negative voices and toxic relationships need to be evaluated?

- Have you created a space in your life for the voice of the Lord?

- Are you tracking prophetic words about your destiny?

- Are you spending strategic times listening and chronicling what the Father is saying to you?

Chapter 6

THE MYSTERY OF FAVOR

Favor is God's primary instrument of promotion. Anytime promotion comes to your life, favor will be the catalyst. Many people do not understand this mystery. Favor can cause one person to arise while another person remains where they are. Favor can cause a door to open, which a person is not at all qualified for in the natural.

> You will find favor and good understanding in the sight
> of God and man. Trust in the LORD with all your heart,
> and lean not on your own understanding; in all your
> ways acknowledge Him, and He will direct your paths.
> —PROVERBS 3:4–6

This Scripture passage reveals two dimensions of favor that each of us needs to fulfill our mandate in the earth. Favor with God and favor with man. Favor with God causes the attention of the Lord to be turned toward you. When you have heaven's attention, you have its promotion and economy.

Graham Cooke writes in his *Brilliant Perspectives* blog:

> Favor is a lifestyle of ever-increasing, ever-expanding
> preference that upgrades our relationship with the
> Godhead and our status in the Kingdom.
> The development of favor goes hand-in-hand

with learning the art of walking out and working in the truth of who Christ is for us and who we have permission to become in Him.

Favor is best received as part of a joyful process that enables us to contend against our own negativity, and overcome every circumstance of life because we have found favor in the eyes of God.[1]

FAVOR RELEASES RESOURCES

Heaven has no resource issues whatsoever. Many believers have been wrongly taught in this area. We must properly understand that God has no lack! There will never be a board meeting in heaven to decide how to pay the bills. Provision is in full supply, and we can tap that supply through our understanding of Abba Father as our provider. We look to Him to sustain, guide, and provide. There really is no clearer picture than God's original plan for man. When He created Adam and Eve, their primary job description was just to fellowship with Him.

> The LORD God planted a garden in the east, in Eden, and there He placed the man whom He had formed. Out of the ground the LORD God made to grow every tree that is pleasant to the sight and good for food. The tree of life was also in the midst of the garden, along with the tree of knowledge of good and evil.
>
> A river flowed out of Eden to water the garden, and from there it parted and became four rivers. The name of the first is Pishon; it encompasses the whole land of Havilah, where there is gold. The gold of that land is good; bdellium and the onyx stone are there. The name of the second river is Gihon; it encompasses the whole land of Cush. The name of the third river is

Tigris; it goes toward the east of Assyria. The fourth
river is the Euphrates.

The Lord God took the man and put him in the
garden of Eden to till it and to keep it.

—Genesis 2:8–15

God placed man in a garden created as a place of beauty for
him. He desired fellowship with His creation. The garden was
watered by a river that split into four rivers and flowed forth.
God went to great lengths to care for man, to custom create a
place of both beauty and provision.

Toil never became a part of man's vocabulary until the fall
(when Adam and Eve disobeyed God and broke covenant). Toil
was the result.

And to Adam He said, "Because you have listened to
the voice of your wife and have eaten from the tree
about which I commanded you, saying, 'You shall not
eat of it,' cursed is the ground on account of you; in
hard labor you will eat of it all the days of your life."

—Genesis 3:17

Hard labor came as a result of man's disobedience. This
was a breach in the relationship with the Father. We have
been restored to a place of relationship, grace, and abundant
provision. The spirit of religion wants to block this truth about
God and His goodness in our lives. It wants to instill rejection
and self-reliance. The spirit of the age wants us to believe that
we have to take care of ourselves and there is no role for God
to provide.

Don't get me wrong. I value a strong work ethic, motivation,
and wisdom! God teaches those values throughout His Word.
Time and again He communicates the rewards of diligence
and faithful stewardship. He also provides insight concerning

sowing and reaping and the importance of both our actions and decisions.

At the center of my relationship must be the truth that God is good, and His desire is to bless me! This frames my decisions and mindset. This truth empowers me to rest as a son knowing that Father has it mapped out. The vivid light of this truth empowers me to conquer fear and rise in faith. It empowers my heart to soar on the winds of dreaming and believing. It allows my mind to be at peace, knowing God's plans and abilities are far higher than mine.

> You are good and do good; teach me Your statutes.
> —Psalm 119:68

Not only is God good, but all that He does is good. His nature contains unparalleled goodness.

> Oh, give thanks unto the Lord, for He is good, for His mercy endures forever!
> —Psalm 107:1

His goodness lasts forever and does not fade! He is merciful and kind to His children.

> The Lord is good to all, and His compassion is over all His works.
> —Psalm 145:9

He is good to everyone! The goodness of God is intended to touch every life. His mercy, His tenderness, and His love are for all who will receive it. He desires to display His love to us.

The goodness of God leads men to lasting and enduring change. The goodness of God acts as a catalyst of transformation and reveals the nature of Jesus and the power of His Spirit.

> Do you despise the riches of His goodness, tolerance,
> and patience, not knowing that the goodness of God
> leads you to repentance?
> —ROMANS 2:4

He has stored up goodness for us! The longer we live, the greater the opportunity to discover His good nature, His good plans, and His good thoughts toward us. As we journey with Him, we are daring to plunge into His goodness with the exuberance and tender childlike faith it takes to receive His heart.

> Oh, how great is Your goodness, which You have laid
> up for those who fear You, which You have done for
> those seeking refuge in You before people!
> —PSALM 31:19

Once I comprehend the love of the Father and His value for me, I am empowered to believe for His favor. I can receive His lavish goodness and life-changing kindness.

> For the LORD God is a sun and shield; the LORD
> will give favor and glory, for no good thing will He
> withhold from the one who walks uprightly.
> —PSALM 84:11

He will not withhold His favor from those who serve Him. Favor is a manifestation of His goodness. A believer who does not accept the reality of God's goodness becomes paralyzed in the area of favor. They simply are unable to access favor; it becomes blocked by lies and a religious mentality.

Many people become trapped at a level of kingdom function far beneath God's destiny for them. They believe God is mighty and powerful, but they stumble over the way they believe He views them. They know God can use anyone and can pick up a nobody and make that person a somebody. They know God can cause His favor to shine and open wonderful doors. They accept those truths, but they do not believe God will do it for them.

I imagine every man or woman who has been wonderfully blessed by God has had to deal with this issue. I know that in my life there have been times I have had to pause and dive into the knowledge of the goodness and love of God so I could fully embrace the things that God had spoken to me.

The heavenly perspective is one without natural limitations. One of the most vivid examples of God's abundance is the vision of John the Revelator in Revelation 21. The streets he saw in the New Jerusalem were made of transparent gold. He saw massive and valuable gems. God spared no expense in His building program!

> The wall was built of jasper and the city was pure gold, as clear as glass. The foundations of the wall of the city were garnished with all kinds of precious jewels. The first foundation was jasper; the second, sapphire; the third, chalcedony; the fourth, emerald; the fifth, sardonyx; the sixth, sardius; the seventh, chrysolite; the eighth, beryl; the ninth, topaz; the tenth, chrysoprase; the eleventh, jacinth; and the twelfth, amethyst. The twelve gates were twelve pearls, each of the gates made of a single pearl, and the street of the city was pure gold, transparent as glass.
>
> —REVELATION 21:18–21

God grants His people favor with man. He causes the right people in the right positions to like you. He causes those who have the keys to your next level to give you access. This is not based upon works but upon His goodness and glory in your life.

Favor will cause what would typically take years to instead happen overnight. I remember several years ago God led me to create a television show. I was excited, but I simply did not have all the resources I needed. One of the areas I lacked was production staff. I needed skilled people to help me launch.

I came across a man who owned a television company and produced for a major cable channel. I reached out to him and inquired about his services and his skilled team. Unfortunately his price was far above my budget at the time. But when I prayed about it, God granted me favor. The man told me he didn't know why, but he felt led to help me. I still remember warning the crew that I spoke in tongues, cast out devils, and prophesied. I wanted them to know what they were getting into when they would be filming me.

They were an amazing fit for my life during that season, and they helped me fulfill a big dream. It was a manifestation of God's favor in my life. God took me far beyond my financial limitations of that season.

In most situations favor is much more valuable than money because it will cause things to happen that money cannot buy. In that particular situation I ended up ministering to the owner of that company and had a wonderful time. God brought me into his life for a cause. Favor aligns you with the right people at the right time.

In all cases when God leads you to a seemingly impossible vision or dream, favor will be His choice weapon. He will cause you to find favor with the needed people at the exact time that you need it. Never listen to the voice of the adversary screaming your destruction. God's favor will abort his lies.

FAVOR RELEASES SOLUTIONS

> Now the boy Samuel was growing both in stature and
> favor with the LORD and also with men.
> —1 SAMUEL 2:26

Samuel was called to shift the course of history in his day. God raised him up at the chosen time. The backdrop was one void of prophetic ministry and revelation. It was a time when the word of the Lord was hard to find in the land.

> Now the boy Samuel was ministering to the LORD
> before Eli. And the word of the LORD was rare in
> those days. There was no vision coming forth.
> —1 SAMUEL 3:1

As is the case with most reformers, Samuel was born in both a difficult and opportune time. He was the answer to an existing problem. This runs parallel to Jochebed and Moses. The Jochebed anointing rises to meet the challenge of the day; it births deliverance.

Samuel was born into the earth with massive prophetic potential. His mother, Hannah, fought a tough fight just to conceive him. This is yet another parallel to Jochebed and the attack on Moses. Hannah refused to give up! She was not only fighting to conceive, but she was also fighting to birth a prophetic general tasked with building and establishing a prophetic culture in the earth. The greatest seeds face the most challenging levels of warfare. This is why it is vital to be equipped to stand, overcome, and prevail.

Notice the two dimensions working in Samuel's life as God groomed him for this task. He was growing in favor with God and man. He needed God to favor him so that His presence and power would be in rich supply. As a prophetic builder he needed God's wisdom to reveal plans and strategies.

Samuel also needed favor with man. He would go on to establish prophetic schools. He required places to host them, as well as teams and leaders. He needed pupils—sons and daughters. God would grant these things into his hands by way of favor!

Favor is a mystery to many because when it comes, it creates rapid acceleration. You simply cannot fulfill God's plan for your life without favor. You cannot buy or earn favor. You cannot manufacture or create favor. The force of favor is in the control of heaven. What you can do is access favor! Favor is accessible through revelation.

Worship Attracts God's Favor

One of the first steps to favor is worship! Worship attracts the presence of God, and where His presence is, there is favor. The true meaning of worship is surrender. Surrendered men and women lift their hands, raise their voices, bow low, and are not afraid to look foolish!

Radical lovers don't care if they are misunderstood. They are not ashamed to express their affection. Worship is a tool of expression. Worship releases heartfelt adoration to the Father.

Worship communicates gratitude and thankfulness. Starting a good worship session is easy. Simply think on one good thing God has done and begin to thank Him right then! It will start a full-blown worship encounter.

> Through Him, then, let us continually offer to God the sacrifice of praise, which is the fruit of our lips, giving thanks to His name.
>
> —Hebrews 13:15

Worship unlocks favor! When a man or woman decides to live in the presence of God and make daily surrender a priority, they unlock favor. I am convinced in reading the story of David that this was one of his master secrets. He was a highly flawed man in many areas, yet he enjoyed miraculous promotions and defense.

David loved to worship! He found healing, safety, and wholeness in worship. He took refuge in the secret place. Time and again he took shelter in the presence of God. In fact David so loved worship that God viewed him as a man after His own heart.

> When He had removed him, He raised up David to be their king, of whom He testified, saying, "I have found David the son of Jesse, a man after My own heart, who will fulfill My entire will."
>
> —Acts 13:22

After the disobedience of Saul, God appointed David to lead Israel. He saw qualities in David that reflected His ways and nature. I believe worship was at the heart of this.

When we worship God and come into His presence, we become saturated with His glory. We reflect the nature of the Father as we are transformed in His presence. David was humble and forgiving because of the presence of God. David had a heart for God's people.

You cannot hang out with Jesus and not become like Him! Over and over we see that people who choose the wrong friends and influences in their lives end up struggling. When we choose the presence of God, we are transformed.

David was after God's heart. He pursued it, and I believe his pursuit attracted God's favor. Your pursuit will also attract God's favor for your life.

GIVING RELEASES GOD'S FAVOR

Giving unlocks favor! When we give to God and to His people, it attracts the favor of God. Giving is reflective of the character and nature of God. The daring offering of Solomon and the gifts of Cornelius brought the attention of heaven to bear on their situations. Their seeds acted as a catalyst for the release of unusual favor. In the case of Cornelius, God moved upon the heart of Peter to minister to him. We could say that this is a manifestation of favor. Peter's attention was turned to the family of Cornelius—favor in motion.

Giving unlocks harvest. Part of that harvest is the manifestation of favor with God and man. When we give to the Lord, we are expressing our trust in Him and His plans. We are rising above our own understanding and accessing heaven's provision.

Heeding prophetic words and instruction will bring both prosperity and favor to your life. When you listen to the voice of God and the leading of His Spirit, you will be led into prosperity.

> Believe in the LORD your God, so shall ye be established; believe his prophets, so shall ye prosper.
> —2 CHRONICLES 20:20, KJV

Let favor be your catalyst today. Expect favor! Decree favor! Access favor! As favor shows up to enlarge and expand you, enjoy it and never apologize for it. *The favor of God is a part of your inheritance.*

PROPHETIC PRAYER

Father, I thank You for uncommon favor in my life. I decree that I have favor with You and favor with man. I love Your presence, and in the midst of Your presence, favor shows up. Thank You, Lord, that Your favor surrounds me like a shield. I am supernaturally sustained and promoted by favor. The right people like me. The right doors open to me. The right opportunities come to me. I walk in immeasurable and supernatural favor in every area of my life, in Jesus' name. Amen.

MY DECREE OVER YOU

I decree miraculous favor in your life. I decree divine opportunities and expansion. I decree that your purpose springs forth in the midst of favor. I decree that God's glory and presence invade your life, and favor comes forth. I decree that you have abounding favor with God and man. God is leading you, directing you, and bringing you into the good land. God is promoting you and placing you. God is guiding you and providing for you, in the mighty name of Jesus. Amen.

POINTS TO CONSIDER

- Do I have a strong revelation of God's goodness in my life?

- Have I believed the lies of the enemy concerning God's view of me?

- Have I believed the lies of the enemy concerning God as my provider?

- What areas of my life need increased favor?

- In what areas of my life is God's favor shooting up? (This is a clue to your destiny. God marks your path with favor.)

Chapter 7

THE MYSTERY OF EGYPT

GOD USED UNCLEAN people and systems in the preservation and raising of Moses. This was God's answer to the prayers of his mother, Jochebed. In God's sovereignty He can choose and use anyone for His purposes. In this chapter we will delve into this concept.

God spared the life of Moses despite a death decree issued by Pharaoh. A proclamation had been issued that all male Hebrew babies were to be killed. The spirit of murder was invading the land through the demonic actions of its leader, Pharaoh. In other words, Pharaoh was operating under demonic power, intent on enslaving the people of God.

Moses was born as God's answer to the cries of a broken people. He was brought into his generation as an instrument of divine deliverance. This is the reason for the warfare surrounding the birth and life of Moses. The enemy was trying his best to snuff him out before he even began.

God had another plan! This is one of the mysteries of the Jochebed anointing and how it relates to your destiny. God can use difficult seasons, difficult places, and even plans of the enemy to become an intricate and vital part of your development.

> And his brethren also went and fell down before his
> face; and they said, Behold, we be thy servants.

And Joseph said unto them, Fear not: for am I in the place of God? But as for you, ye thought evil against me; but God meant it unto good, to bring to pass, as it is this day, to save much people alive. Now therefore fear ye not: I will nourish you, and your little ones. And he comforted them, and spake kindly unto them.

And Joseph dwelt in Egypt, he, and his father's house: and Joseph lived an hundred and ten years.

—GENESIS 50:18–22, KJV

ENDURING ATTACKS

Joseph's story is that of another man in Egypt saved by God for a divine purpose. Joseph was sold into slavery by his brothers. This wicked betrayal forced him into a land filled with idolatry and divination. He survived miraculously to become the premier leader, warning Pharaoh of impending doom.

Three elements of this story parallel the story of Moses.

First, despite adversity and a terrible set of circumstances, the purpose of Joseph's life prevailed. We can gain strength and encouragement from this story. Many times we face dreadful attacks and have to rise above them. Two things the enemy sows into our minds are fear and discouragement. He will lie to us and tell us that our purpose is derailed.

Many believers simply give up during these types of attacks. Yet there is a bigger picture here. The consummate creative genius mapped out the plan for your life. Your present situation might look insurmountable, but God is the Master of the comeback! He can and will move in your situation—if you refuse to give up.

The LORD is my light and my salvation; whom shall I fear? the LORD is the strength of my life; of whom shall

I be afraid? When the wicked, even mine enemies and
my foes, came upon me to eat up my flesh, they stum-
bled and fell. Though an host should encamp against
me, my heart shall not fear: though war should rise
against me, in this will I be confident. One thing have
I desired of the LORD, that will I seek after; that I may
dwell in the house of the LORD all the days of my life,
to behold the beauty of the LORD, and to enquire in
his temple. For in the time of trouble he shall hide me
in his pavilion: in the secret of his tabernacle shall he
hide me; he shall set me up upon a rock.

—PSALM 27:1–5, KJV

David authored this psalm. He understood setbacks, attacks,
wilderness seasons, and trials. He boldly declared that he
would not fear his enemies. He knew that God had sealed the
plan for his life and that His power would indeed preserve him,
and it did!

David had tremendous confidence in the Lord even though
he faced repeated difficulties. Time and again he went right
back to God, and God's power lifted him. This lesson must be
learned in order to walk out the plan for your life. You might
find yourself in the deepest pit like Joseph, or in the toughest
struggle like Moses, or in the most terrifying confrontation
with a giant like David, but in all those moments, God's plans
and thoughts toward you are unwavering.

He has not changed His mind. His power is still alive and
active in your situation. It takes this kind of thinking, this
mindset of champions, to make it to the other side of the storm.

In the case of Joseph, God's power was working during each
negative trial. He was wrongly punished, yet time after time
he bounced back and thrived. God is really good at justice and
purpose.

> The LORD shall judge the people: judge me, O LORD, according to my righteousness, and according to mine integrity that is in me.
>
> —Psalm 7:8, kjv

God's judgment supersedes that of man. I have often seen people do deceptive and dishonest things. They may get away with it for a brief period, but eventually the justice of the Lord will be administered. Believers must rely on this principle.

> Judge me, O LORD, for I have walked in my integrity. I have trusted in the LORD; I will not slip.
>
> —Psalm 26:1

God's justice acted on behalf of Joseph. He walked uprightly before the Lord, so God defended and protected him. God used favor and justice as divine weapons in the life of Joseph.

Second, the Lord used each and every plot twist to form Joseph for his great future purpose and impact.

> Likewise, the Spirit helps us in our weaknesses, for we do not know what to pray for as we ought, but the Spirit Himself intercedes for us with groanings too deep for words. He who searches the hearts knows what the mind of the Spirit is, because He intercedes for the saints according to the will of God.
>
> We know that all things work together for good to those who love God, to those who are called according to His purpose. For those whom He foreknew, He predestined to be conformed to the image of His Son, so that He might be the firstborn among many brothers.
>
> —Romans 8:26–29

Most preachers quote verse 28 to explain away tragic things or adverse circumstances. It definitely applies to the life of Joseph as it demonstrates the ability of God to weave a glorious tapestry from the most tattered fabric. The passage in Romans is connected to praying in the spirit. As we allow Holy Spirit to pray for us and reveal the mind of God, we tap into realms of intercession and insight that equip us for each and every situation.

What Joseph's brothers intended for evil, God turned around for good! This is the power of purpose in our lives. The enemy can throw the most awful thing at us, and God still finds a way to use it for good. We must be careful not to blame God for things devised by the enemy. Just because it happened doesn't mean that God authored it.

The enemy has a clear-cut mandate. All destruction and evil come from him.

> The thief does not come, except to steal and kill and destroy. I came that they may have life, and that they may have it more abundantly.
>
> —JOHN 10:10

God the Father has good gifts. When His fingerprints are on our lives, we see grace revealed and love manifested.

> Every good gift and every perfect gift is from above and comes down from the Father of lights, with whom is no change or shadow of turning.
>
> —JAMES 1:17

Third, God used Joseph in the midst of a wicked place, and He further used a wicked place to provide for him. This is the mystery of Egypt. God uses people, places, and situations that we deem off limits. We must be open to the possibility of an

Egypt in the formation of our destiny. It was evident also in the story of Jochebed.

The Jochebed anointing is one that brings preservation and protection. The Jochebed anointing taps into divine favor in the midst of wickedness. Moses' very name spoke of the role that a wicked kingdom would play in his safety and development.

> Now the child grew, and she brought him to Pharaoh's daughter, and he became her son. And she called his name Moses and said, "Because I drew him out of the water."
>
> —Exodus 2:10

Moses was drawn out of the Nile, a place known for idolatry. He was miraculously delivered from the decree of death. He was taken into the system of Egypt and raised there. God knew exactly what He was doing!

Unconventional Plans for Unconventional Deliverance

It was an unconventional plan, but God was in it. As I am penning these words, I hear the Lord saying, "Tell My people to look out for My unconventional plans. Get ready for unconventional deliverance. Get ready for unconventional provision. I am going to use people in your journey that you never thought I would use. I am going to bring provision from unlikely sources. I am going to draw you out of adverse circumstances and set you in the midst of destiny. You will bring glory to Me. I will use you to reveal My glory in the midst of wicked places."

Egypt, one of the oldest civilizations in history, became a place of both refuge and oppression. The culture of Egypt was dominated by false gods and demonic symbolism.

> Now there was a famine in the land, so Abram went
> down to Egypt to live there, for the famine was severe
> in the land.
>
> —Genesis 12:10

Mysteriously God used this unclean land as a place of refuge in the lives of several of the Bible's most prominent Old Testament figures. For example, Abraham (Abram) retreated to Egypt during a time of famine. Yet his wealth increased in the land of Egypt, and he learned vital technologies of the day from the Egyptian people, who were proficient in the art of well digging and irrigation. God used ungodly people and an ungodly place to bless, protect, and enrich the life of the father of faith.

> So Abram went up from Egypt to the Negev, he and
> his wife and all that he had, and Lot with him. Abram
> was very wealthy in livestock, in silver and in gold.
> He continued on his journey from the Negev and
> came to Bethel, to the place where his tent had been
> at the beginning, between Bethel and Ai, to the place
> where he first made an altar. There Abram called on
> the name of the Lord.
>
> —Genesis 13:1–4

This passage gives vital clues to the mystery of Egypt in the life of a world changer. Abraham went by the leading of the Lord into an unclean place. He went to a place under the leadership of ungodly people, yet God moved in his life in that place. I believe God is calling many people to bless you and assist in your development—people who may not fear or know your God, but they have been assigned to be a part of your story. Do not be shocked when God prompts people who are not serving Him to bless you or contribute to the mandate upon your life.

Many are being prepared to go into realms and segments of

the marketplace, government, entertainment, education, politics, media, and various other places of society and make a kingdom impact. They must understand how to handle Egypt. They must understand that they are called to be a kingdom ambassador in Egypt. Egypt will not define them; they will redefine Egypt.

Abraham lied and created a mess in Egypt. This was one of his character flaws and a curse that would show up again in his family lineage. Even when Abraham blew it, God showed up in power and preserved his wife and family.

Abraham enjoyed abundance in a wicked place! He thrived in a place where people were ungodly. He also built an altar! This has profound prophetic significance. Abraham carried the place of worship and presence with him. He was not in Egypt to let them define his moral code; he was in Egypt on assignment! Egypt had a role to play in his story, but he was still sold out to Yahweh. This is the difference maker. We are called to carry the presence everywhere we go and have kingdom influence. We are called to be living expressions of the kingdom of God. We are not called to learn the ways of people who do not fear or worship God.

The lesson to learn from the lives of Jochebed, Moses, and the other figures we have referenced is the uncanny ability of God to use unlikely people, places, and sources in the development, funding, and launching of our destiny. Never count out the possibility that God is going to use someone whom you would never choose. He can put His hand on anybody and cause that person to bless you. You are to be obedient and follow His leading no matter where it takes you.

PROPHETIC PRAYER

Lord, I embrace the unusual and unconventional development of my destiny. I will not be afraid of unexpected places and people in my life. I trust You and choose to follow Your leading every step of the way. I thank You that You are working all things for my good. I thank You that You are turning around every trap and plot of the enemy. I thank You that You are causing men and women to bless my life and sow into my destiny, in the name of Jesus. Amen.

MY DECREE OVER YOU

I decree supernatural leading and provision in your life. I declare places of refuge and increase. I decree that God is causing people to sow into your development and growth. I decree unusual benefactors in your life. I decree underwriters. I decree forward motion and momentum, in the name of Jesus. Amen.

POINTS TO CONSIDER

- Is God leading me to unusual people or places?
- Is God calling me to be a kingdom ambassador in the midst of a seemingly wicked place?
- Am I open to God leading me to unlikely places?

- Am I conscious and aware of the opportunity to represent and reflect the kingdom everywhere I go?

- Am I able to navigate through ungodly areas of society while keeping my morals intact?

- Do I have a firm conviction of biblical values and living?

- Am I open to the uncommon and the unusual?

Chapter 8

THE MYSTERY OF THE GLORY

Moses is one of the exceptional glory carriers in biblical history. God used His glory in the work of deliverance, birthed through Jochebed. This chapter will explore the beauty, majesty, and mysteries of the glory of God, as well as teach why glory is essential to supernatural destiny.

I will never forget a night in the glory of God that marked me forever. Before I share this story with you, let me preface it by saying that wild and uncommon things happen in the glory of God. On this particular night a tangible manifestation of glory came into a revival meeting in which I was ministering. These were no ordinary meetings. They were unplanned, extended meetings birthed in response to an unusual measure of hunger in the people with God's glory showing up!

I was on the platform with some other ministers when the weighty presence of God showed up. We were having difficulty standing and functioning. It felt as though we were in another realm, because we were! Suddenly I saw what I call the "lightning of God." His glory and His healing power were there. It felt tangible to me in one exact area on the stage.

As the glory increased, I asked for deaf people to come. I felt that God wanted to open the ears of the deaf that night. As soon as they came forth and stood in that area on the stage, ears began to pop open with ease. There was no effort. The glory was doing it! The glory was manifesting, and miracles were taking place.

Aside from the fact that the healings were happening so easily, I also noticed the unusual way that it seemed to be in one spot. It was as though a little heaven bubble opened up! Now before you start correcting my theology on this, let me say that I fully understand that we carry the kingdom in us, and the glory of God is available everywhere. I do believe that there are some New Testament examples of glory breaking out in particular places.

> God worked powerful miracles by the hands of Paul. So handkerchiefs or aprons he had touched were brought to the sick, and the diseases left them, and the evil spirits went out of them.
>
> —ACTS 19:11–12

Paul had captured both revelation and tangibility of the kingdom. If the sick could just get where he was, they could step into the manifest glory he was carrying. It was easy to get healed! When the glory shows up, it is so easy to get healed. For those who could not get to the meetings, they asked for cloth that had been in contact with Paul's earthly body. They wanted a piece of something that had been in that atmosphere. This was so they could make contact with the glory.

GLORY CARRIERS

> But we have this treasure in earthen vessels, the excellency of the power being from God and not from ourselves.
>
> —2 CORINTHIANS 4:7

As New Testament believers the kingdom has been fully invested and established in us. We are carriers of glory, power, and the governmental authority and power of heaven. When we show up, power, glory, and authority show up. Demons have no choice but to flee.

We need to learn to maximize the glory. We need to learn to seek it out and set the stage for it in our personal lives and corporate gatherings. I remember when a minister I know began to say that God spoke to him about glory gatherings. He prophesied that we would have glory gatherings where the body of Christ would encounter the glory of God in uncommon ways. There is something about gathering in a corporate setting and engaging the glory realm.

> When you discover things that seem to contribute to the glory, do those things more; and when you find things that seem to diminish the glory, stop doing them. It's as simple as that.[1]
>
> —Ruth Ward Heflin

This is simple advice! If you want the glory, find out what brings it and live there. Live in the glory zone. Live in the place that pleases God. Find out what brings the glory and maximize it. Find out what pleases God, and do it. Find out what God doesn't like, and avoid it. These are basic yet profound nuggets of wisdom.

It is impossible to discuss Jochebed without diving deep into the mystery of the glory. The Jochebed anointing births glory and deliverance. In the midst of the glory realm bondage is shattered, yokes are destroyed, and ailments are healed.

After the great glory carrier Moses had stepped out prematurely and fled, a glory encounter brought him back into purpose.

> Now Moses kept the flock of Jethro his father-in-law, the priest of Midian, and he led the flock to the far

side of the desert and came to the mountain of God, to Horeb. The angel of the LORD appeared to him in a flame of fire from the midst of a bush, and he looked, and the bush burned with fire, but the bush was not consumed. So Moses said, "I will now turn aside and see this great sight, why the bush is not burnt."

When the LORD saw that he turned aside to see, God called to him from out of the midst of the bush and said, "Moses, Moses."

And he said, "Here am I."

—EXODUS 3:1–4

The voice was coming from the midst of the flame. God's voice resides in His glory. The fire and the glory housed the voice of God and caused Moses to leave his old life of refuge to rise into the anointing of a deliverer.

Glory will forever mark you. You cannot come in contact with the glory of God and remain the same. Many times, in our limited human minds, we define the glory as only one dimension of God's presence, but the glory is far more than that. I have met people who think that the glory is only a still, small voice; a quiet moment; or a knockdown encounter that leaves you laid out on the floor. While all these things can happen in the glory, it can take on so many other attributes. The glory can show up with thunder or as a loud, emanating reflection of the voice of Yahweh. It can even show up as a burning fire. Never limit the flow or reach of the glory.

And I lifted up my eyes, and I saw a man with a measuring cord in his hand. And I said, "Where are you going?"

And he responded, "To measure Jerusalem and to note what is its width and length."

Then the angel who was speaking with me went out,

and then another angel came out to meet him, and said to him, "Run, say to this young man: Jerusalem will be inhabited as villages without walls, because of the multitude of men and animals in her. And I will be like a wall of fire all around her, says the LORD, and I will be as glory in her midst."

—ZECHARIAH 2:1–5

The Lord was dealing with His people and the city of Jerusalem. He said that He would surround the city with fire and glory. The fire and the glory go together. Fire burns out the impurity and brings forth the purposes of God. It ignites passion for His presence and denies desires of the flesh.

ANGELS AND GLORY

Wherever there is glory, there are angels! The angel in the passage from Zechariah was helping to administrate the plans and purposes of God. Expect angelic intervention, appearance, and protection as you press into the glory of God. Angels are assigned to the servants of Yahweh. We should never become so fascinated by angels that we confuse their position or rank, but we should also learn to work with angels. Angels have been assigned to people, territories, and mandates.

Then the LORD said to Moses, "Depart, go up from here, you and the people whom you have brought up from the land of Egypt, to the land which I swore to Abraham, Isaac, and Jacob, saying, 'To your descendants I will give it.' I will send an angel before you, and I will drive out the Canaanite, the Amorite, the Hittite, the Perizzite, the Hivite, and the Jebusite. Go up to a land flowing with milk and honey. However, I will not go up in your midst, for you are a stiff-necked people, and I might destroy you on the way."

—Exodus 33:1–3

The Lord told Moses that as he went and brought the people forth, a warring angel would clear the land. Angelic armies have been assigned to the people of God. They've been tasked with enforcing heavenly mandates and plans, and assisting with the intent and will of heaven. They are God's supernatural agents of enforcement.

INTIMACY BRINGS THE GLORY

Moses took the tent and pitched it outside the camp, a good distance from the camp, and called it the tent of meeting. And anyone who sought the LORD would go out to the tent of meeting which was outside the camp. So whenever Moses went out to the tent, all the people would rise up and stand, every man at the entrance of his tent, and gaze after Moses until he entered the tent. And whenever Moses entered the tent, the pillar of cloud descended and stood at the entrance of the tent, and the LORD spoke with Moses. When all the people saw the pillar of cloud standing at the entrance of the tent, all the people rose up and worshipped, every man at the entrance of his tent. The LORD spoke to Moses face to face, just as a man speaks to his friend. When he returned to the camp, his servant Joshua, the son of Nun, a young man, did not depart from the tent.

—Exodus 33:7–11

God would meet with Moses face to face. No separation existed between Moses' friendship with God and the assignment God had given him. This is a real key. All too often we compartmentalize our mandate and our relationship with God. We focus on the what, the where, and the how, but we forget about the who. The real quest of Christianity is to know the King. Doing the kingdom without intimate personal knowledge of the King is spiritual corruption.

Daily the King is pursuing your heart and affection. He is waiting for you to arise and give Him your attention. A love relationship flows from a redeemed heart, not from a routine of works and striving.

It is challenging to adequately describe the glory of God with limited human understanding and terminology, but one of my descriptions is "proximity to Him and His presence." To me the glory is only experienced up close, honest, and raw.

You cannot be polished in the glory. You cannot be professional in the glory. You just have to be tender, available, and longing. The longing heart is fulfilled and satisfied in the glory. The longing heart pants as the deer for the water. The longing heart tunes in and listens for the voice of the Master. The longing heart does not make a ritual out of prayer, fasting, or seeking God; instead, they become a free-flowing lifestyle. There may be set times and purposes for pursuit, but hosting the presence of God becomes a natural extension of the longing heart.

Moses was sent as a leader filled with glory. What would happen if our ministers carried passionate hearts filled with glory? What would our churches look like if they hosted the glory? What would our cities look like if they bowed beneath the weight of His glory? What would our nation look like with blazing glory carriers heralding the King in all His glory? May a glory-filled generation arise at this time.

> Moses said to the LORD, "See, You say to me, 'Bring up this people,' but You have not let me know whom You will send with me. Yet You have said, 'I know you

by name, and you have also found grace in My sight.'
Now therefore, I pray You, if I have found favor in
Your sight, show me now Your way, that I may know
You, and that I may find favor in Your sight. Consider
too that this nation is Your people."

And He said, "My Presence will go with you, and I
will give you rest."

—Exodus 33:12–14

God told Moses that He would go with Him! Where you
find the glory, you find God Himself. He wants to go with us
into every assignment. Moses pursued the Father. Those who
pursue Him will carry the weight of His glory.

God said that His presence would be with Moses and that
he would have rest. When you move in the glory realm, you
are not exhausted or frustrated. Frustration comes when you
attempt to fulfill heavenly mandates through the arm of the
flesh. When you stay in the place of glory, and the presence is
with you, there is refreshing and joy, strength and peace, and
protection and provision.

Then Moses said, "I pray, show me Your glory."

Then He said, "I will make all My goodness pass
before you, and I will proclaim the name of the Lord
before you. I will be gracious to whom I will be
gracious and will show mercy on whom I will show
mercy."

—Exodus 33:18–19

Moses had an earnest request; he wanted to see the glory of
God! He did not want merely to *tell* the people about God's
power and deliverance; he wanted to *see and experience* the
glory of God. The pursuit of God's glory causes it to manifest
in your life.

God said He would cause His goodness to pass by Moses. God is a good God. Goodness and kindness are a part of His nature. You cannot be near to the glory of God without experiencing the goodness of God.

GLORY BRINGS INCREASE

Out of the midst of the glory comes promotion. This is one of the intriguing aspects of glory. People arise in the midst of glory. Purposes arise in the midst of glory. Enlargement and expansion burst forth from the glory realm.

> Arise, shine, for your light has come, and the glory of the LORD has risen upon you.
> —ISAIAH 60:1

You cannot abide in God's glory and stay small! Increase comes in the glory realm. Favor breaks forth in the glory realm. Expect promotion when you come into the glory of God. Expect solutions and answers when the glory of God shows up in your life. God is unlimited. His thoughts are expansive, and His plans are mega. When you encounter the glory realm, you exit the limitations of humanity and enter the dimension of divine enlargement.

The Hebrew word for *glory* is *kabod*, which means heaviness or weight. This definition is tied to biblical prosperity. Gold and silver are weighed to determine value, and they are connected to the glory realm.

> And I will shake all the nations, and they will come with the wealth of all nations, and I will fill this house with glory, says the LORD of Hosts. The silver is Mine, and the gold is Mine, says the LORD of Hosts. The glory of this latter house will be greater than the

former, says the LORD of Hosts. And in this place I
will give peace, says the LORD of Hosts.

—HAGGAI 2:7–9

GLORY COVERS

Then the LORD will create over all of Mount Zion and
over those who assemble there a cloud of smoke by day
and a glow of flaming fire by night; over everything the
glory will be a canopy.

—ISAIAH 4:5, NIV

There is a realm of heavy glory that forms a canopy. It acts as
a protective covering over the people of God. The glory canopy
can cover regions and ministries. Under this canopy attacks
from hell can be thwarted and unusual protection can manifest.

When Moses was receiving the law of God, he had a glory
encounter. God's glory covered him and swept him up in the
cloud of presence. From that place, he received the revelation
for that dispensation. I wonder how many revelations we miss
because we do not live more intentionally focused on the glory.
Abiding in the glory is an effective deliverance strategy. You
remain shielded and protected under the cloud!

Another word associated with glory is *shekinah*. It means
"'dwelling' or 'one who dwells.'"[2] The shekinah glory of God is
associated with the tangible manifestation of the glory of God.
It is the brilliance and radiance that comes in the midst of the
people of God. It is the dwelling of the cloud of His presence.
When the shekinah shows up, God's radiant presence is upon us!

Chayil is a Hebrew word often associated with the glory of
God. It means power, wealth, and strength. The glory brings
chayil.

> Through God we shall be valiant, for He shall tread
> down our enemies.
>
> —Psalm 108:13

In this verse the word *valiant* is the word *chayil*. God strengthens us and gives us the victory! When Moses led the children of Israel, they experienced the kabod of God (heavy glory), they experienced the shekinah of God (brilliant glory), and they experienced the chayil of God (wealth, strength, and force). God anointed Moses in the midst of His glory. God equipped Moses in the midst of His glory.

Israel was led by the cloud and the pillar of fire. They were supernaturally charged and led. This is the picture of God's equipping for destiny in our lives. They came out of bondage healed and increased with prosperity. The chayil showed up in their lives, and God reversed the plans of hell!

PROPHETIC PRAYER

Thank You, Lord, for Your glory in my life. I cry out to You for Your glory. I thank You for Your radiance in my life. I thank You for Your brilliance in my life. I thank You, Lord, for Your might in my life. I thank You, Lord, for the fire and the glory surrounding every area of my life. I pray today, Lord, that You show me Your glory, in Jesus' name. Amen.

MY DECREE OVER YOU

I decree God's glory over your life. I declare that you are led forth by glory. I declare that the chayil of God shows up in your life. I declare that wealth and increase is yours. I declare that force and favor are yours. I declare that angels are on assignment to protect and assist you. I decree that you hunger for the glory of God. I decree that you see, know, and experience the brilliance of Jesus. I decree that you are a glory carrier. You move in the glory of God. You walk in the glory of God. You live in the glory of God. Glory surrounds you. Glory covers you. Glory radiates from you. Glory guides you. You love the glory of God and release it everywhere you go, in Jesus' name. Amen.

POINTS TO CONSIDER

- Am I sensitive to atmospheres and realms?
- Do I pray for and expect the glory of God?
- Have I allowed the fire of God to purify me?
- Do I recognize when the glory of God rushes in?
- Am I really a glory carrier, manifesting heaven wherever I go?
- I must learn to be open to unusual manifestations in the glory.
- I need to spend time daily in God's presence to know the glory realm.

Chapter 9

THE MYSTERY OF DELIVERANCE AND DELIVERERS

MEN AND WOMEN are entrusted with the assignment of deliverance in the earth. When God decides to address a problem in humanity, He anoints men and women to arise and meet the challenge. This is impossible in and of our own strength. It takes the power of God in operation.

> And it shall come to pass in that day, that his burden shall be taken away from off thy shoulder, and his yoke from off thy neck, and the yoke shall be destroyed because of the anointing.
>
> —Isaiah 10:27, KJV

The anointing is the power and presence of God to fulfill the mission and mandate. It is God's super on your natural. God never tasks people for kingdom purpose without anointing them. The anointing is God's explosive power to equip, excel, and fulfill. Anointed people can do impossible exploits. Anointed people can break through where others have failed. Anointed people can achieve seemingly impossible objectives. Anointed people can tear down and uproot demonic systems and bondage.

Yoke-Destroying Power

In Isaiah we receive a weighty prophetic picture. The anointing is described as a yoke-destroying force. To more fully understand this description, we must dig deeper into what a yoke is. Jochebed was destined to birth deliverance. She was also raising and guiding a deliverer. Many people fight battles based upon the anointing on their life to set others free. This chapter will teach on the vital need for supernatural deliverance and the challenge that all deliverers will face.

A yoke is an instrument that binds two oxen together for the purpose of plowing. In the spiritual sense this was pictured as a burden and the tie to the burden. People who are "unequally yoked" (2 Cor. 6:14) to an unbeliever are those in covenant relationships with unbelievers. They have formed a tie that creates spiritual damage in their lives.

We can become yoked to demonic entities and practices. The yoke represents bondage.

> Therefore, you will serve your enemies whom the Lord will send against you, in hunger, thirst, nakedness, and need of all things, and He will put a yoke of iron on your neck until He has destroyed you.
> —Deuteronomy 28:48

The yoke mentioned here is the result of spiritual disobedience. It was a warning to Israel of the danger of rebellion and refusal to honor their covenant with Yahweh. The anointing destroys the yoke! It obliterates the tie to demonic oppression. It sets people free. There is nothing quite like the anointing and the power of God's deliverance.

I remember a night that God used a team to free a young lady who had come up for prayer. As we began to pray for her, it became clear that a demonic spirit was operating through her. Her voice changed, her mannerisms changed, and she was doing what we call "manifesting," meaning the spirits were reacting to the power and authority of God. People with demons will manifest when the anointing shows up or when authority is present. Demons hate the life and freedom that comes with the anointing, and authority will expose demons every time.

That lady had been severely bound by demons. My team prayed and prayed for her, peeling back layer after layer of oppression. The struggle was so significant that I asked them to take her into the back while I continued to minister to the crowd. When the meeting ended later that night, I went into the back room where they were still casting devils out of her. I joined them, and we ministered to her some more.

Finally, we got to the root cause, and I had her renounce some things. We knew this was the key, but it was literally a fight to get that woman to be able to speak and silence the demons. We eventually got there, and the breakthrough came! It was a mighty battle. The demons put up a strong fight that night, but we persisted and kept standing on the authority of Jesus and the Word of God.

A few years later her pastor called me to tell me that she and her family were in his church. Prior to her deliverance their lives were a wreck, but her whole attitude and mindset changed after she was set free. Some of her family would not even go to church before, but when they saw the change that occurred in her, they wanted to check it out. She is free today and serving in ministry in that church. God changed her life! Deliverance will change your life forever.

It is worth the fight and the labor involved to see a soul set free! Deliverance is messy. It can be exhausting and difficult, but it is desperately needed. Wonderful people throughout the nations are called of God, but they need yokes destroyed, demons cast out, and mindsets changed. Many churches are too proper to engage in the ministry of deliverance. They do not cast out devils. They are ashamed of that part of the gospel. Thank God, Jesus did not feel that way.

> They went to Capernaum, and immediately on the Sabbath He entered the synagogue and taught. They were astonished at His teaching, for He taught them as one having authority, and not as the scribes. In their synagogue there was a man with an unclean spirit. And he cried out, "Leave us alone! What do You have to do with us, Jesus of Nazareth? Have You come to destroy us? I know who You are, the Holy One of God."
>
> Jesus rebuked him, saying, "Be silent and come out of him!" When the unclean spirit had convulsed him and cried out with a loud voice, it came out of him.
>
> They were all amazed, so that they questioned among themselves, "What is this? What new teaching is this? With authority He commands even the unclean spirits, and they obey Him." Immediately His fame spread everywhere throughout the region surrounding Galilee.
>
> —MARK 1:21–28

The man was sitting right there, in the midst of all types of religious people, yet he was demonized. He was bound up, but he only received help when Jesus came into the room. The religious people were shocked because this level of faith and authority was uncommon. Religious people don't like deliverance. They don't like taking authority over demons.

Jesus Is a Deliverer

Today entire movements shun the ministry of deliverance. Some of the leaders of these groups are deceived, teaching and believing erroneous things as they make fun of casting out demons. They do not realize that they are making fun of one of the primary ministries of Jesus. He loves to set people free!

Derek Prince wrote about this passage in his book *They Shall Expel Demons*:

> First Jesus dealt with the demons, not with the man. The demon spoke out of the man, and Jesus spoke to the demon. Literally translated, what Jesus said to the demon was, "Be muzzled!"
>
> Second, Jesus expelled the demon from the man, not the man from the synagogue.
>
> Third, Jesus was in no way embarrassed by the interruption or disturbance. Dealing with the demon was a part of His total ministry.
>
> Fourth, the demon spoke in both singular and plural forms: "Did You come to destroy us? I know who you are..." (verse 24). This response is charac-teristic of a demon speaking for itself and on behalf of others. The demon in the man in Gadara used the same form of speech: "My name is Legion; for we are many" (Mark 5:9).
>
> Fifth, it is reasonable to assume that the man was a regular member of the synagogue, but apparently no one knew that he needed deliverance from a demon. Perhaps even the man himself did not know. The anointing of the Holy Spirit on Jesus forced the demon out into the open.
>
> Sixth, it was this dramatic confrontation with a demon in the synagogue that launched Jesus into His

113

public ministry. He became known to His fellow Jews first and foremost as the Man with unique authority over demons.[1]

Deliverance was front and center in the ministry of Jesus. He boldly combatted demon powers with strength and authority.

> God anointed Jesus of Nazareth with the Holy Spirit and with power, who went about doing good and healing all who were oppressed by the devil, for God was with Him.
>
> —ACTS 10:38

You cannot deal with the devil through weakness, timidity, and fear. These elements attract demonic powers. Believers must know their authority and enforce it over the powers of darkness.

You cannot sing a demon out. You cannot will it out, laugh it out, or shake it out. You must *cast* it out! Casting out devils is the finger of God manifested in the lives of bound people.

LEVELS OF DELIVERANCE

There are levels of deliverance and deliverers:

+ **personal deliverance**—from little, tormenting demons

+ **regional deliverance**—working within a territory to enforce the kingdom and to combat ruling spirits

+ **national deliverance**—combatting the spiritual climate over a nation and breaking the grip of a demonic prince

- **global deliverance**—releasing prophetic instruction to the nations and arming the *ekklesia* to arise in freedom

The various levels require different revelations, spheres of authority, and strategies. It takes a different strategy to work within a region than to deal with an individual. You are also dealing with varying levels of demons.

Moses was raised by God in answer to the bondage of the Hebrews. A deliverer is born with unique purpose, unusual power (of the Spirit), uncommon faith, perseverance, and solutions. God empowers ordinary men and women to do extraordinary exploits. Moses was one such a man.

> Now therefore, the cry of the children of Israel has come to Me. Moreover, I have also seen the oppression with which the Egyptians are oppressing them. Come now therefore, and I will send you to Pharaoh so that you may bring forth My people, the children of Israel, out of Egypt.
>
> —Exodus 3:9–10

God heard the cries of His people. He saw their oppression, and He met the need with the birth of a deliverer. Jochebed carried in her womb the answer to the conflict and bondage. Amazingly God chooses to partner with men and women to fulfill His mandates in the earth. He chooses to send His people forth and equip them to bring freedom.

The Marks of a Deliverer

Uncommon wisdom

God grants insight and wisdom in the areas of your destiny. You have something woven into the fabric of your identity that will bless and help others. It may seem a small thing, but it will become a big blessing to someone. Deliverers are given wisdom. God gives them insight and ability. He gives them plans and strategies. (See Proverbs 4:5.)

Uncommon encounter

God will encounter you and reveal Himself to you. When He was ready to send Moses, He met him in a supernatural encounter. When God assigns a man or woman, He arranges extraordinary encounters with that person.

Uncommon revelation

Revelation provides access to God's mind and plans. He mantles us for deliverance and destiny by granting us His insight. He desires to unveil secrets and mysteries to us. Deliverers expose others to freedom by manifesting the mind of God.

Uncommon power

The Bible is a book of miracles. God never sends a person without power. Deliverers access unusual power.

Uncommon obstacles

The life of a deliverer will be opposed and resisted because the enemy is trying to shut down the mission before it begins. If Satan weren't alarmed, he would not attack.

Uncommon tenacity

Deliverers have no quitting sense. They get knocked down, but they get back up. Hell may throw you a body blow, but you have resurrection living in your belly. There is a bounceback somewhere in your spirit (Prov. 24:16).

Uncommon solutions

Moses had answers because he heard from God. God is the wisest Being in existence. When we have been with Him, we will have uncommon answers for problems.

Uncommon journey

Every twist and turn prepares the life of a deliverer. The uncommon journey holds keys and lessons.

Uncommon breakthrough

Deliverers have a breakthrough anointing. They have been tasked and mantled with breakthrough. They are not held down by the powers of hell. Freedom is their portion.

PROPHETIC PRAYER

Father, I thank You for the understanding and revelation of freedom in my life. I recognize that where Your Spirit is, there is liberty. I am not ashamed of deliverance, and I know that You have granted me authority over demonic opposition and bondage. I confess that I live free. My mind is free. My body is free. My home and family are free. I submit and surrender to Jesus Christ; therefore, I walk in supernatural life and freedom, in Jesus' name. Amen.

MY DECREE OVER YOU

I decree victory and freedom in your life. I declare God's delivering power to be upon you and within you. I release the Spirit of almighty God in your life.

I decree that everywhere you go, freedom goes. I say that you carry deliverance and freedom in your life. You are anointed to set the captives free, in the name of Jesus. Amen.

POINTS TO CONSIDER

- Do I walk in freedom in every area of my life?
- Have I allowed the spirit of fear to hinder my assignment?
- Have I sought the Lord for deliverance from any yokes?
- What things have I quit that I need to start again?
- Am I faithful to pray for insight into my destiny?
- Am I a deliverer? Do I manifest freedom to others?

Chapter 10

THE MYSTERY OF BIRTHING

Now I want to explain an important law of the kingdom: all significant things must first begin as seeds. The enemy comes after the seed because the seed breaks demonic cycles. There is a painful birthing process for kingdom purposes and plans. The enemy does all that he can to get people to give up while they are still in the gestational process. This chapter will reveal keys to help you to stand and endure the birth pains, as well as emphasize the importance of birthing.

As we have already established throughout this book, everything in the kingdom begins in seed form. This is one of the areas where the enemy tries to run rampant in our minds. He will challenge how small our dreams look, how insignificant we are, how tiny our breakthroughs seem. He does all of that to attempt to get us to give up and retreat. He wants us to abandon the seed so that the harvest never comes. In many ways the devil has more faith in our destiny than we do. He sees the potential and fights hard against it.

He knows that what God has planted on the inside of you is a threat to his evil plans. He knows that if you pray and obey God, you will be an instrument of destruction to the plans of hell. Jesus has commissioned us to terrorize hell.

> Whoever practices sin is of the devil, for the devil has been sinning from the beginning. For this purpose the Son of God was revealed, that He might destroy the works of the devil.
>
> —1 JOHN 3:8

Jesus came to tear down the kingdom and structures of hell. He has anointed us to be ambassadors for the kingdom of God. Part of that commission is to wage war on the devil's schemes and operations. We are called to make hell miserable. We have never been called to be miserable!

A significant key to moving in destiny is to understand birthing. God plants something on the inside of you for an appointed time. He leads you daily to prepare your heart and reassure you that He is still moving in your life. He gives you baby steps to pursue the plan for your life. Then suddenly, major doors open and breakthrough comes, but it all begins with a seed.

CAN YOU HANDLE A SEED?

God provides the seed, but we provide the womb. Our lives must be fertile places for the kingdom of God to be planted and grow. We steward the dreams, visions, small promptings, and huge desires, keeping our hearts planted in Him so His promises can be fulfilled in our lives.

> Delight yourself in the LORD, and He will give you the desires of your heart. Commit your way to the LORD; trust also in Him, and He will bring it to pass.
>
> —PSALM 37:4–5

This is one of my favorite promises in Scripture! If I delight myself in the Lord, if I live a life planted in loving Him and knowing Him on an intimate basis, then He promises to give me the desires of my heart. He promises even to meet the little requests. This means that I can see Jesus in the small daily breakthroughs and in the big earth-shattering miracles. I can see Him all around me. I can see Him leading me and guiding me. I can see Him gently nurturing my heart and leading me forward.

Another truth relates to this promise. What happens when my heart does not align with His? I believe this verse speaks of the progress of committing my way (my journey) to Him. As I pursue Him, my heart is being transformed and renewed. The word for *heart* used in the New Testament indicates it is related to the center of thought, reason, and decision making. Simply put, the more I walk with Jesus, the more that I begin to think and dream like Him. Let's look at some applicable promises in that area.

> For My thoughts are not your thoughts, nor are your ways My ways, says the LORD. For as the heavens are higher than the earth, so are My ways higher than your ways, and My thoughts than your thoughts.
> —ISAIAH 55:8–9

These verses inspire and challenge me! They reveal the Father's desire to elevate my thinking so that I can enter the realm of the impossible and supernatural. All too often my mind is stuck in low gear, but when I hang out with God, He invites me into higher thinking, bigger dreaming, and daring realms of faith.

> Let this mind be in you all, which was also in Christ Jesus.
> —PHILIPPIANS 2:5

Jesus never dangles a promise in front of us that we can't walk out. He is good, and He does not lie! In the verses that follow this promise, He lays out His mind by speaking of humility and surrender. He is inviting us into a lifestyle of surrender that frees our minds from fear, lack, and limitation. We can think on another level and then move on another level.

Being invited to think like the Lord is a critical part of birthing. We must be able to see the big picture and not complain or grumble. Complaining kept the children in the wilderness for an entire generation. An entire generation missed their destination because of their negative attitude. This is toxic!

Complaining is the fruit of unresolved discouragement and bitterness. It is the release of toxic emotions. It establishes open doorways to demonic bondage keeping us stuck in places where we were not intended to remain. In fact, typically when you are ministering deliverance to someone in bondage, you must get them to go back and break negative decrees they have made. You must lead them through renunciations to break every agreement with hell.

> Neither murmur, as some of them also murmured and
> were destroyed by the destroyer.
> —1 Corinthians 10:10

The word *murmur* here means, "to utter secret and sullen discontent, express indignant complaint, murmur, grumble."[1] The enemy sows seeds of bitterness and defeat. He wants to captivate your thought life to get your mouth saying the wrong things. Complaining is the enemy's attempt to get you prophesying destruction over your life. Hell plans to create a disruption in your harvest. You will not birth the destiny that God has intended for you while yielding to murmuring. You must renew your mind and get control of your mouth. Your mouth is an instrument of power. Every time you open it, you are either blessing or cursing!

> Out of the same mouth proceed blessing and cursing. My brothers, these things ought not to be so. Does a spring yield at the same opening sweet and bitter water?
> —JAMES 3:10–11

This verse reveals the power of the tongue. James is stating that as believers we should use our mouths as pens of blessing, not as objects of destruction. We should live with redeemed minds and therefore redeemed speaking. We really can change the world around us through the words of our mouth. We can also water the seed and birth the promise of God with our words.

Jochebed became pregnant with a promise of deliverance. She was carrying a cycle-breaking seed. The enemy fought all that he could to keep this baby from growing up and coming into his mantle as a deliverer. She not only bore him but nurtured and protected him as she followed God's plan.

> God blessed them and said to them, "Be fruitful and multiply, and replenish the earth and subdue it. Rule over the fish of the sea and over the birds of the air and over every living thing that moves on the earth."
> —GENESIS 1:28

God commanded Adam and Eve to be fruitful and to multiply. God planned to populate the earth with a generation that would seek His face and walk with Him. His mandate for humanity was to conceive and birth!

Keys of Birthing

Recognize the law of seed.

This is a spiritual law that governs the kingdom. You must have your eyes open to the reality that you are constantly living in the realm of sowing and reaping. Your life right now is manifesting the harvest of previous seeds.

You have given up on some seeds you've sown! The enemy caused weariness to set in and aborted your harvest. You must live intentionally, give intentionally, pray intentionally, study intentionally, and move in the kingdom intentionally.

Water the seed.

The kingdom grows in your personal life in stages. First, the blade (praise God for the little things—despise not the day of *small* beginnings). Then, the ear (a little fruit). Next, the *full fruit* (power and wonders). Finally, the harvest—the fruit—begins to affect others, and the kingdom is enlarged and expanded.

Prophesy.

The prophetic spirit speaks life to dead things. The prophetic spirit sees into the invisible realm. When we prophesy, we are declaring the mind of God over situations. We are declaring the mysteries and wisdom of God. We are also preparing ourselves for effective battle and overcoming.

Stay in the presence of God.

Time and again Israel waged and won wars by the presence of God. They defeated their enemies by following the presence of God. The presence of God strengthens you. The presence of God empowers you. The presence of God encourages you.

Travail.

Every seed is intended to culminate in a birth. Travailing is a realm of prayer where you give yourself over to deep and intense prayer to release what God has placed within your spirit.

> My little children, of whom I labor in birth again until Christ is formed in you.
>
> —GALATIANS 4:19

Paul knew how to labor and birth! Birthing is essential for destiny. He was determined to pray the will of God through for His spiritual children.

> Who has heard such a thing? Who has seen such things? Can a land be born in one day? Can a nation be brought forth all at once? As soon as Zion travailed, she also brought forth her sons.
>
> —ISAIAH 66:8, NASB

When Zion (the people of God) travails, she brings forth sons! Certain seeds will not come forth without intense and dedicated prayer. We will look at travail more at the conclusion of this chapter.

Break the spirit of barrenness.

Everything God created is designed to be fruitful. Barrenness is not the plan of God. We saw God's command to Adam and Eve as revealed in Genesis 1, and He has not changed His mind. He wants His people to be prosperous and moving in kingdom multiplication.

The spirit of barrenness aborts plans and purposes. It endorses and orchestrates premature launches. It wants to shut down kingdom growth and momentum.

The spirit of barrenness will create toil without fruit. Laboring and seeing no results will breed exhaustion and frustration. This is the plan of this spirit: to get believers to give up.

The spirit of barrenness will attempt to rob the harvest. It comes to attack the seed and block the harvest.

The spirit of barrenness tries to block church and ministry growth. This spirit will literally sow seeds of strife and confusion to keep the church from growing. Many leaders are facing the spirit of barrenness in their ministries.

Historically the birth of prophets has been attacked. The enemy tries to take them out before they are even born. The spirit of barrenness will do its best to annihilate prophets and prophetic people in regions and ministries. It wants to abort the operation of the prophetic.

Embrace the day of small beginnings.

When a seed is planted, it begins as a small thing. This concept is revealed in Scripture by the parable of the mustard seed. The mustard seed is one of the smallest seeds, yet there are mustard seeds all over the world. The size of the seed does not determine the potential of the harvest! The tree can grow in various types of soil, including those in which it is difficult to produce crops. It is a remarkably resilient seed. Mustard trees can become towering, shade-producing trees that grow up to twenty feet tall and wide. The leaves produce mustard. The tree has a variety of uses. This enormous tree sprouts from a tiny yet mighty seed!

> And the Lord said, "If you had faith like a mustard seed, you would say to this mulberry tree, 'Be uprooted and be planted in the sea'; and it would obey you."
> —Luke 17:6, nasb

Your big harvest begins as a little seed! Do not stumble over the small beginning. Instead, discern the greatness wrapped in the tiny seed.

Heed prophetic warnings.

Prophetic warnings can save your life, your assignment, and your family. I will never forget a time when my wife and I were in a meeting, being invited into a ministry relationship that seemed like a great idea at the time. In the midst of the meeting I heard the Lord whisper, "Lies," down deep in my being. I struggled at first to discern whether it was in my mind or my spirit. When I shared with my wife, she said she had heard the exact same thing! We knew that God was warning us. We did not enter the agreement, and some years later we knew why. It is a long story, but the Lord saved us a multitude of sorrows with His warning. One warning can rescue your purpose. Don't overlook it!

Refuse to give up.

There will be countless opportunities to quit! Quitting is easy. Anyone can give up. It takes guts, perseverance, and stamina to go all the way. Champions refuse to quit. They stare adversity in the face and fight. The Lord will empower you to stay strong if you seek Him.

Birthing requires conception.

Prophetic planting: God plants His purposes in your spirit! What has God spoken to you? What have trusted people in your life discerned concerning your purpose? These are indicators of what you are called to birth.

Birthing requires intimacy.

You cannot give birth to kingdom purposes without a life-style of intimacy with the King. The *what* is not more important than the *who!* This thing is about a man named Jesus. Keep Him in focus with a lifestyle of daily surrender and seeking.

Birthing requires care.

You have to steward your destiny. Grow in knowledge. Study, plan, and prepare. The birthing room speaks of an atmosphere. Webster's dictionary states one of the definitions for *atmosphere* is "a surrounding influence or environment."[2] We are significantly impacted by environments. Hospitals work to create safe and comfortable places for new mothers to give birth. Create a place of inspiration and prayer in your home. Create a place that fuels your vision. Atmospheres are realms of creativity. Things are birthed, released, stirred, and deposited in atmospheres. Attitudes—and the expression of those attitudes—set the emotional temperature of an atmosphere just like a thermostat sets a natural temperature. Sights and sounds help create atmospheres. Changing the sights and sounds around you can change your atmosphere.

Birthing is connected to travail.

Intercessors open wombs! Travail releases the realm of birthing in the spirit. What has been closed opens and is filled with new life.

In an article published on *Elijah List*, James Goll writes:

> "What is travail?" These prayer approaches have been a "Lost Art" in the body of Christ, but in the current move of God, old ways are being made new. Let me try to explain it.
>
> As it is in the natural, so it is in the spiritual. Travail is a form of intense intercession given by the Holy Spirit whereby an individual or group is gripped by something that grips God's heart. The individual or

group labors with Him for an opening to be created so that the new life can come forth....

Travail takes place after you have carried something in your heart for some time, but it comes on you suddenly....Later the strategic time comes to push that promise forth through the prayer canal. Finally you realize that the promise has been born, and you are greatly relieved when the delivery is over!

The prayer of travail is God desiring to create an "opening" to bring forth a measure of life or growth. If the "opening" was already in place, there would not be the need for travail. Just as the "opening" of the natural womb is enlarged to bring forth the baby, so travail creates an "opening" or "way," whereas before the opening or way was closed. With travail, there is always a way opened for life, newness, change, or growth."[3]

Surely you are familiar with the Bible story of Elijah and the rain. One aspect of this story pertains to travail and birthing. Elijah had seen the rain and heard the sound. He was taken into a realm in the spirit where rain was more real than drought. In the natural realm the land was as dry as a bone.

Prophets do not move according to natural times, seasons, or logic. This is because they are God's mouthpieces, and God is not confined by these things. He rules over them! Elijah heard the rain, felt the rain, and spoke existence to the rain. He then sent his servant Gehazi to look for the cloud. But I want to pay attention to the posture of the prophet during this event.

Elijah said to Ahab, "Get up, eat and drink, for there is a sound of a heavy rainfall." So Ahab got up to eat and drink. And Elijah went up to the top of Carmel, and he threw himself down on the ground and put his face between his knees.

—1 Kings 18:41–42

Elijah was in the birthing position! He was partnering with the word of the Lord. He understood that his prayer was able to bring the word into the earthly realm. You must be willing to carry the seed, water it, protect it, and birth it. It will produce that which God said. As Elijah prayed, the rain came!

In the meantime, the sky turned black with clouds and wind, and there was a great rain. And Ahab rode and went to Jezreel.

—1 Kings 18:45

Your life and destiny might look dry today, but I want to announce to you that heaven has rain clouds to water your seed! Heaven has glory storms to multiply what has already been planted. Learn the art of travail and pray it forth. *It is yours!*

PROPHETIC PRAYER

Lord, I thank You for the small things in my life. I see and discern the seeds that have been planted. I thank You that I am a wise steward over the seeds in my life. I thank You that I obey You and hear the warnings You speak to me. I thank You that I see the clouds of rain to water the seed. I thank You that I am an intercessor and know how to birth and travail. I decree that I will bring forth good fruit in my life, in Jesus' name. Amen.

MY DECREE OVER YOU

I decree growth and expansion in your life. I release the spirit of prayer. I say that you pray and obey. You see and hear, then move accordingly. I decree that you are not stuck. You heed prophetic warnings, you steward prophetic words, you refuse to complain. You move under the timing and direction of heaven. You birth the plans and purposes of God. You do not get off the birthing table. You are faithful to see the plan of God all the way through to completion, in the name of Jesus. Amen.

POINTS TO CONSIDER

- Have I been faithful to travail and birth my destiny?

- Do I pray and listen for God's direction?

- Have I allowed the spirit of barrenness to steal my seed?

- Do I pursue intimacy with my Father?

- Do I heed the prophetic words and warnings spoken over me?

- I must vow to germinate my seed with prayer, worship, and intimacy.

Chapter 11

THE MYSTERY OF PROTECTING EMERGING SEED

S EED MUST BE protected, but many people do not know how to guard and preserve their prophetic destiny. This chapter will give you keys and practical advice to protect your seed. It will also build faith for divine protection.

As we have already established in this writing, everything in the kingdom begins in seed form. We take a step of faith, believing that we will receive a harvest. God plants His dreams of significance deep within our hearts, and we rest, knowing we have heard His voice clearly. Then we take a step to fulfill what God has called us to do.

The journey of Jochebed and Moses is full of divine protection against the many plots of the adversary. We must understand that the enemy will work overtime to pluck up the fragile seed before it even begins to germinate. Emerging seed is fragile and must be protected.

I remember when I faced an attack of the enemy trying to pluck up the seed from my young heart. I had received the call of God for ministry and was ready to take my first step of faith. I was about to embark on the most significant journey of my young spiritual life. I was going to leave everything I knew to head on a grand adventure.

It took every ounce of faith I had to be brave enough to say yes. I was saying yes to relocating. I was saying yes to leaving my family and support system. I was saying yes to a huge financial step of faith. I was saying yes to the unknown! I was taking the plunge because I knew I had heard from God.

In the middle of this decision-making process, the enemy tried to pluck up the seed. Someone who had been very instrumental in my salvation process began to speak negative word curses over my decision. This person told me I was making a huge mistake, that I would fail, and that God had not called me to ministry. I was so shocked because this person had been a big part of my salvation story. Now, suddenly, the person was coming against the plan of God for my life!

Looking at it now, I can see it clearly. This person simply did not want me to leave, so in the moment of frustration, he allowed the enemy to use his mouth. The word curse was powerful. But I ignored what was spoken over me, and instead chose to believe the prompting I felt to go on this excellent adventure. I had to rise above my emotions, my mind, and the warfare that had been perpetrated against me.

WAR THROUGH PEACE

I have learned through the years that warfare around big decisions is not uncommon. In these moments we must tune into the Lord to find the deep, abiding peace. I look for that peace. I know that if I am obeying God, He will provide a tangible peace. Peace surrounds obedience. Your mind can be bouncing in a million directions, but your spirit will be at rest when you are in the middle of the will of God.

Let peace be your umpire. Let peace confirm the will of

God for your life. Let peace be a directive and move with the peace of God.

> Do not be anxious or worried about anything, but in everything [every circumstance and situation] by prayer and petition with thanksgiving, continue to make your [specific] requests known to God. And the peace of God [that peace which reassures the heart, that peace] which transcends all understanding, [that peace which] stands guard over your hearts and your minds in Christ Jesus [is yours].
> —PHILIPPIANS 4:6–7, AMP

Believers have access to peace the world knows nothing of—a peace that passes mental comprehension, a peace that can at times be totally disconnected from the natural world. This peace is not circumstantial; it does not come and go based on your surroundings. It is rooted in knowing God, trusting God, and obeying God. This peace is a magnificent gift in your life. It is the secret sauce of obedience. The road of Christianity may be extremely narrow and sacrificial at times, but at the end of the day there is majestic peace. The peace of God is incomprehensible and will keep you in rest.

I had peace about my decision despite the word curses. I went to Bible college and began a glorious adventure of faith. Every destiny will demand a faith adventure. Why? Because we learn to trust God in the rugged places of obedience. In those times of stepping out without having all the answers, we find the glory of God. When we find the glory of God, we will be supernaturally sustained.

Many of my Bible college days were full of opposition and struggle. The enemy would tempt me to quit. He was trying to pluck up the emerging seed in my life. He was trying to abort the mission Jesus had sent me on. On those days when the temptation to quit would be tangible, I could again hear those negative, cursing words. They were ringing in my ear, urging me to give up. The enemy was giving me a list of excuses for why my obedience was crazy.

In truth, my saying yes to this journey was crazy! It did not make natural sense. I was on a daring adventure of obedience to the call and mandate of God. I was moving beyond my comfort zone. I was launching out into the deep.

> A man's heart devises his way, but the LORD directs
> his steps.
>
> —PROVERBS 16:9

God was directing my steps. He was healing me, delivering me, and preparing me to go to nations. At the same time, the devil was trying to pluck up the seed. He was trying to stop my progress. After several experiences with discouragement and the recurrence of those words, I rose in faith and broke the curses. I used my authority as a believer to break every curse that had been spoken over me.

This is a critical step in protecting your seed. At that time in my life, I did not have the base of knowledge that I do now. I did not realize the power of words, because if I had, I would have taken authority over the evil decree much sooner. Now I am quick to break curses spoken over me. I do not do it from a place of fear but from a place of power and authority. Jesus has given us authority in the realm of the spirit!

War From Heavenly Places

> For He rescued us from the domain of darkness, and transferred us to the kingdom of His beloved Son, in whom we have redemption, the forgiveness of sins.
> —Colossians 1:13–14, nasb

We have been translated or transferred from one *place* to another. We have been taken from one realm to another, moved from one dimension to another. The sacrifice of Jesus at the cross paid our debts fully and transferred us from the domain (rulership and authority) of darkness into the marvelous power and rule of Jesus! We are now fully active citizens of His kingdom, called to dwell in a new dimension.

> And you were dead in your trespasses and sins, in which you formerly walked according to the course of this world, according to the prince of the power of the air, of the spirit that is now working in the sons of disobedience. Among them we too all formerly lived in the lusts of our flesh, indulging the desires of the flesh and of the mind, and were by nature children of wrath, even as the rest. But God, being rich in mercy, because of His great love with which He loved us, even when we were dead in our transgressions, made us alive together with Christ (by grace you have been saved), and raised us up with Him, and seated us with Him in the heavenly places in Christ Jesus, so that in the ages to come He might show the surpassing riches of His grace in kindness toward us in Christ Jesus.
> —Ephesians 2:1–7, nasb

In verse 6 of this passage the word *heavenly* is the Greek word *epouranios*, meaning "heavenly, celestial, in the heavenly sphere, the sphere of spiritual activities; met: divine, spiritual."[1] *Places* here is a word that means in, on, or among; again, it denotes a location. The picture is that we have been removed from a kingdom or *place* of darkness and brought into the place or space of the kingdom of God. Again, this is speaking of a realm, not a time or season.

> Therefore if you have been raised up with Christ, keep seeking the things above, where Christ is, seated at the right hand of God. Set your mind on the things above, not on the things that are on earth. For you have died and your life is hidden with Christ in God.
> —COLOSSIANS 3:1–3, NASB

We combat the powers of hell from a place of victory and authority. The enemy was successfully stripped of all rule in our lives. We can break each curse that hell tries to proclaim against us. We act as the agency of the kingdom, ruling and reigning on earth. We do not operate from fear or defeat but from a place of strength and victory.

WAR AGAINST WORD CURSES

> How will I curse whom God has not cursed? Or how will I defy whom the LORD has not defied?
> —NUMBERS 23:8

This verse asks a straightforward question, "How can a man curse what God has already blessed?" The answer is we cannot. This is where we get our strength in rising against word curses.

What is a word curse? Let's begin with the definition of the word *curse*, which, according to Oxford's online dictionary, is "a solemn utterance intended to invoke a supernatural power to inflict harm or punishment on someone or something."[2]

Everything in the spirit realm is created and established by words. God creates by words. The enemy establishes demonic powers and influence by words. Prophets and prophetic people release spiritual utterances, speaking words that build, create, and establish. The mouths of prophets are instruments of building. Believers operate in kingly authority as we declare and proclaim. This is the mission of God's sons and daughters. Our mouths are gateways.

Let's look at these scriptures about the power of the tongue.

> A fool's lips enter into contention, and his mouth calls for flogging. A fool's mouth is his destruction, and his lips are the snare of his soul. The words of a talebearer are as wounds, and they go down into the innermost parts of the body.
>
> —Proverbs 18:6–8

> Death and life are in the power of the tongue, and those who love it will eat its fruit.
>
> —Proverbs 18:21

> My heart is inditing a good matter: I speak of the things which I have made touching the king: my tongue is the pen of a ready writer.
>
> —Psalm 45:1, kjv

How can we effectively break a word curse? The first step is recognizing it. Are any negative words spoken over you trying to pluck up the seeds God has planted in your life? Has anyone ever made any demonic pronouncements over your life, family, or ministry? Discern the curses. Once you have seen the hand of the enemy at work, you must break it. You break it by renouncing it. You use the words of your mouth, empowered by the Holy Spirit through the authority of Jesus, to declare those word curses null and void. Break all association with those word curses. Boldly declare that those words are ineffective, and cut every tie in the realm of the spirit. Then confess the Scriptures! Find a Scripture verse or verses that apply to the area in which you were cursed. Speak the blessing of God over your life. Speak the Word of God. If a curse of sickness was released by someone, speak healing verses and command your body to receive the life of God. When you release the blessing, the curse must fall.

Many voices will try to speak to you, to either empower your seed or hinder it. You must use discernment to heed the right voices while cutting off the wrong ones.

> "Truly, truly I say to you, he who does not enter by the door into the sheepfold, but climbs up some other way, is a thief and a robber. But he who enters by the door is the shepherd of the sheep. To him the doorkeeper opens, and the sheep hear his voice. He calls his own sheep by name, and he leads them out. When he brings out his own sheep, he goes before them. And the sheep follow him, for they know his voice. Yet they will never follow a stranger, but will run away from him. For they do not know the voice of strangers." Jesus told them this parable, but they did not understand what He was telling them.
>
> —John 10:1–6

Jesus' voice is a clear, consistent gift in the life of a believer. It fuels our seed, arms us for victory, and empowers us to win. He is always speaking, even when we don't feel it. We must learn to tune out the static and listen for His still, small voice speaking truth and clarity over our lives.

Voices We Must Discern

The voice of faith

Faith is a speaking spirit. Listen to the voice of faith in your life. Read, meditate, and speak the Word of God. Release the voice of faith over your seed. Speak and declare what heaven says while shunning what hell says.

The voice of doubt

The enemy will sow seeds of doubt to abort your harvest. He will often have friends and family speak negative things over you. Be quick to recognize the voice of doubt and cut it off. Your friend or family member may not know any better, but make sure you do not come into agreement with the voice of doubt. Stay in faith!

The voice of discouragement

Discouragement comes to rob your courage. Without courage you will struggle to obey God and take bold steps. When the enemy tries to bomb your mind with discouragement, cast those thoughts down.

The voice of accusation

The devil is the accuser of the brethren (Rev. 12:10). He will bring up your past, your mistakes, and all other manner of lies. Be quick to recognize his tactics and pull them down. Stay built up by meditating on the promises of God.

To protect emerging seed, you need some power tools— spiritual weapons to help you turn back the advances of the enemy.

SIX POWER KEYS TO PROTECT YOUR SEED

1. Pray bold prayers!

> Ask and it will be given to you; seek and you will find;
> knock and it will be opened to you. For everyone who
> asks receives, and he who seeks finds, and to him who
> knocks, it will be opened.
>
> —MATTHEW 7:7–8

Praying big, bold, God-sized prayers is key, as well as interceding and praying the mind of God over your life and destiny. Your commitment to pray is imperative in the growth and development of your seed.

2. Be alert!

> Pray in the Spirit always with all kinds of prayer and
> supplication. To that end be alert with all persever-
> ance and supplication for all the saints.
>
> —EPHESIANS 6:18

One tactic the enemy uses to defeat you is to lull you to sleep in a spiritual sense. Praying in the spirit and accessing the mind of God unpacks revelation to arm you for victory. You must be alert to recognize and discern the strategies of hell.

3. Prophesy!

Your tongue was created to release powerful words in the spirit realm. When hell comes after your seed, make war with prophetic utterances and boldly speak what God says. The Lord will send the spirit of prophecy to help build you up.

> But he who prophesies speaks to men for their edifica-
> tion and exhortation and comfort.
>
> —1 CORINTHIANS 14:3

4. Rest!

A rested mind is a peaceful mind. A rested body is able to journey with unshakable tenacity. Rest is a gift, not a weakness. Two types of rest are critical. The first is spiritual rest, which is resting in faith and knowing "it is finished!" The second is natural rest. You must rest your mind and body, or you will grow tired and weary, which makes you more susceptible to the lies of the enemy.

> Come to Me, all you who labor and are heavily burdened, and I will give you rest.
>
> —Matthew 11:28

5. Establish accountability relationships!

You need people in your life who will be bold and honest with you. You need friends and family who love you enough to tell you the truth. You need leadership that challenges you and does not just affirm you even when you are wrong! This is vital. Accountability is protection; it is the tool of winners. Those with longevity have built a team of counselors, friends, advisers, and leaders who speak into their life.

> As iron sharpens iron, so one person sharpens another.
>
> —Proverbs 27:17, niv

6. Adhere to absolute moral standards!

> Woe to those who call evil good, and good evil; who exchange darkness for light, and light for darkness; who exchange bitter for sweet, and sweet for bitter!
>
> —Isaiah 5:20

Forming a nonbiblical moral compass is one of the most dangerous things a believer can do. As disciples of Christ we are called to live out our faith according to the Word of God. The enemy will lure you into gray moral territory through the spirit of the world, carnal wisdom, and perversion. His ultimate goal is to diminish conviction and shipwreck your Christian walk. You must determine to hold fast to biblical truth and base your life on it.

God's remarkable journey of faith for you begins with seemingly small steps! You must pray and tend to the seeds of growth being planted in your life. The next big breakthrough begins with a small seed!

PROPHETIC PRAYER

Lord, I thank You that I am alert, obedient, and on course with You. I break and bind every word curse off my life, in the name of Jesus. I pull down all evil decrees, and I declare that I am blessed. I say that I walk in the glory. I move in the glory. I am following Your path, and I am filled with Your power. I live in tune with You and refuse to cede any ground to the enemy, in Jesus' name. Amen.

MY DECREE OVER YOU

I declare power and strength over you and your seed. I say that destiny is growing in your life. I break any word curses spoken over you. I pray for strong discernment and supernatural understanding in your life. I say that you are not distracted or confused. I decree that you are spiritually alert and ready to fulfill the mandate of heaven upon your life, in Jesus' name. Amen.

POINTS TO CONSIDER

- I need to learn to discern curses and break them off my life.
- I must spend time in prayer and the Word to know the promises of God.
- I need to water the seeds of destiny in my life by studying and preparing.
- I release blessings over myself, my destiny, my family, and my future generations.
- I will have godly relationships with those who speak truth into my life.
- I adhere to godly standards and morals; my moral compass is holy.
- I decree that my seed grows into a mighty ministry, bringing others into the kingdom.

Chapter 12

THE MYSTERY OF WEAKNESS

Tʜɪꜱ ᴄʜᴀᴘᴛᴇʀ ᴇxᴘʟᴏʀᴇꜱ one of the most perplexing mysteries concerning the mind and ways of God. Why would He limit Himself by choosing to operate through simple and often weak human beings? He is God Almighty! He can use anybody or anything, yet He chooses to work in the earth through people. The same people that He created to bring praise and glory to His name have often abandoned and betrayed Him. Yet His love always remains.

The gifted preacher Charles Spurgeon summed it up this way, "Though you have changed a thousand times, He has not changed once."[1]

> So, what do you think? With God on our side like this, how can we lose? If God didn't hesitate to put everything on the line for us, embracing our condition and exposing himself to the worst by sending his own Son, is there anything else he wouldn't gladly and freely do for us? And who would dare tangle with God by messing with one of God's chosen? Who would dare even to point a finger? The One who died for us—who was raised to life for us!—is in the presence of God at this very moment sticking up for us. Do you think anyone is going to be able to drive a wedge between us and Christ's love for us? There is no way! Not

trouble, not hard times, not hatred, not hunger, not homelessness, not bullying threats, not backstabbing, not even the worst sins listed in Scripture:

They kill us in cold blood because they hate you.

We're sitting ducks; they pick us off one by one.

None of this fazes us because Jesus loves us. I'm absolutely convinced that nothing—nothing living or dead, angelic or demonic, today or tomorrow, high or low, thinkable or unthinkable—absolutely nothing can get between us and God's love because of the way that Jesus our Master has embraced us.

—Romans 8:31–39, msg

These verses paint such a profound picture of God's unending love for us. We must understand that love was His motivation, love is His motivation, and love will always be His motivation. His love neither waivers nor expires. His love empowers our relationship with Him. He took the first step by sending Jesus even when we were in rebellion against Him.

Properly understanding the deep and abiding love that the Father has for us is critical in embracing our destiny. God chose Jochebed to birth Moses, who would set captives free! God anointed Moses, then camped out in the midst of His people with glory. No matter what wall Moses came up against, God was there.

Deliverance is a demonstration of love! Love sets captives free. Love tears down demonic walls. Love empowers purpose. God's love in action brought the Hebrews out by the cloud and fire!

The toughest struggle in fulfilling our God-ordained destiny is dealing with our own human weaknesses and flaws. It becomes difficult to believe God can use us when we examine our strengths and weaknesses and our shortcomings overwhelm us. Moses experienced the same thing!

Then Moses said to the LORD, "O my Lord, I am not eloquent, neither before nor since You have spoken to Your servant. But I am slow of speech, and of a slow tongue."

The LORD said to him, "Who has made man's mouth? Or who made the dumb, or deaf, or the seeing, or the blind? Have not I, the LORD? Now therefore go, and I will be with your mouth and teach you what you must say."

He said, "O my Lord, send, I pray, by the hand of whomever else You will send."

The anger of the LORD was inflamed against Moses, and He said, "Is not Aaron the Levite your brother? I know that he can speak well. And also, he comes out to meet you, and when he sees you, he will be glad in his heart. You shall speak to him and put the words in his mouth, and I will be with your mouth, and with his mouth, and will teach you what you must do. What's more, he will be your spokesman to the people, and he will be as a mouth for you, and you will be as God to him. You must take this rod in your hand, with which you will perform the signs."

—EXODUS 4:10–17

God called Moses to speak on His behalf. He was to be God's ambassador, representing His agenda on earth. But Moses had a problem! He had a speech impediment. Most theologians believe that this problem was some type of stutter.

When he argued with God about his condition, the Lord appointed Aaron to go with him. God already has answers and solutions for your mandate. This is part of His mystery. God already knows who and what it will take to accomplish what He has assigned to you. He is just waiting on your yes so He can send everything you need. He is trying to stretch your faith beyond your perceived ability. He is trying to take you into deeper levels of surrender. He already has the right people and resources for your assignment.

Why would God call a man to do the very thing he felt the least qualified to do? Why not call him to do something with his hands or his mind? Why call him to use his mouth when he was unable to speak clearly? These types of questions arise when God breathes His majestic breath upon our lives. He inspires and commissions us to do seemingly impossible things. He declares purpose in the most vulnerable areas of our lives.

The Lord reminded Moses that it was He who made his mouth. He was pointing Moses away from his human weakness and putting the emphasis back on His power. He knew that He was going to surround Moses with His glory and work supernatural miracles through him.

He wasn't looking for Moses' human strength; He was looking for his surrender and his absolute trust. To anoint men and women for extraordinary works, God needs their total reliance. He needs them to look fully unto Him, not to their own abilities or gifts. Many powerful leaders end up shipwrecked when they yield to a spirit of deception and begin to believe the power belongs to them. The power is sovereignly held in the hands of God, released to men and women to steward, but their role is always to point the receivers back to the source.

SURRENDER AND WEAKNESS

A self-reliant, self-promoting man or woman forgets to point people back to the origin! God originated the power, the love, and the grace. The deepest levels of surrender only empower reflection. This is a biblical principle.

Let's look at this through a few scriptures.

Then Jesus said to them, "Truly, truly I say to you, the Son can do nothing of Himself, but what He sees the Father do. For whatever He does, likewise the Son does."

—JOHN 5:19

If you love Me, keep My commandments. I will pray the Father, and He will give you another Counselor, that He may be with you forever.

—JOHN 14:15–16

Worship God! For the testimony of Jesus is the spirit of prophecy.

—REVELATION 19:10

In each of these verses there is a level of surrender and obedience. Jesus boldly declared that He was planted in the Father, and He only did that which He saw the Father do. Many people do not understand this principle, and instead, they bow to the spirit of the age, yielding to the belief that they must strive to get ahead. This is the spirit of the world in operation, and unfortunately it is common in the church. Believers step on one another and trample over others to promote their gifts, their ministries, or their agendas.

Jesus lived a surrendered life, and He had an unending flow of power. Many people want the power of God, but they fail to understand the price. The price is their will. The spirit of prophecy unveils the majesty of Jesus to men and women. Prophetic words and operations should always be pointing people back to the Lord, not to the vessel!

Love empowers surrender and trust. We have become a generation that speaks loudly and shouts our love from the rooftops, but true love is proven through covenant actions. True love is sacrificial. This means giving up a personal desire for the ambition of the one you love. I could not think of a better way to describe the pathway of Christianity. It is a series of surrenders and exchanges.

> Then He said to them all, "If anyone will come after Me, let him deny himself, and take up his cross daily, and follow Me."
>
> —LUKE 9:23

Jesus' description of Christianity was a daily surrender. Part of following Him was an exchange of ideas. We let go of our preconceptions to take on His way of thinking. We quit looking to do our own thing our own way, and instead, we yield to Him. For this reason and others, prayer is the lifeblood of Christian living—we need to be washed in His presence to deal with our hearts and lay down the parts that try to rise against His will. It also allows Him to speak into us and relate fresh vision, hope, and insight for the mandate He has given. Prayer is the fuel of obedience.

> I can do all things because of Christ who strengthens me.
>
> —PHILIPPIANS 4:13

In the passage that leads up to this verse, Paul is describing his journey of highs and lows, victories and attacks, as he served Christ as His apostle. He learned a master key: the ability released in Christ Jesus.

Paul understood the power of covenant. I often describe covenant as a great exchange. We exchange our sin for His righteousness, our brokenness for His wholeness, our infirmity for His healing. Salvation is a great exchange. It empowers us to receive the full benefits of all Christ accomplished at the cross.

We must view destiny through this lens. There is power available by and through Jesus Christ. When God calls us to do anything for Him, He has already provided the power. It is in Him, through Him, and by Him.

God chooses people who are seemingly weak in an area and wraps His strength around them. He sends them to do something they feel unqualified to do. He wants to receive all the glory. If we go on an assignment we feel capable of doing without Jesus, we will not rely upon Him nor give Him glory. God chooses to use us in areas where we have no natural confidence. He aims to testify of His goodness through our lives.

> When they saw the boldness of Peter and John and perceived that they were illiterate and uneducated men, they marveled. And they recognized that they had been with Jesus. But seeing the man who was healed standing with them, they had nothing to say against it.
> —ACTS 4:13–14

Peter and John were so surrendered to Jesus that uncommon power emanated from them! People knew they had been with Jesus because they were moving above and beyond their own natural abilities. This is the evidence of the glory! When the glory moves into your life, you move outside of your typical capacity. God wants to raise people up in His glory. He wants to commission businesses, birth churches, and release revelation in the glory. He wants to shake nations with the glory.

The glory will send you, heal you, and strengthen you. When you know that God is calling you to move beyond your own ability into the arena of His miracle power, you will become dependent upon the glory.

Peter and John reflected the weight of His majesty. Diseases were instantly healed as these two men manifested the presence of Jesus. Surrender carries presence. Surrendered people are presence people, obedient people, uncommon people.

I often see preachers who are wise because of their studies and discipline. They can articulate profound concepts with ease because they have diligently prepared. They are master communicators, and yet many times there is a void of the residue of heaven. There is little or no demonstration of the power of the kingdom. They are functioning in their own strength. What would happen if God challenged them to press outside of their comfort zone, to move into an unknown place? They would have to increase their level of dependence upon God and the measure of the supernatural would exponentially increase.

I believe God is looking for people and places where He can show His strength. I remember when I was new to the ministry, I visited a world-renowned ministry that hosted a daily healing school. I was amazed because people came from the nations to be taught and healed. They came both to hear and see. Such was the biblical ministry of Jesus: people did not just hear; they heard and saw!

> God anointed Jesus of Nazareth with the Holy Spirit and with power, who went about doing good and healing all who were oppressed by the devil, for God was with Him.
>
> —Acts 10:38

Everywhere Jesus went there were miracles. Very few modern preachers have been able to live in such a realm. I know of some because I have studied them in my quest to understand the supernatural. One common thread I have found is that they paid a deep price to walk in such power.

They had to sacrifice their own ambitions and plans. They had to face intense scrutiny from the church, particularly the portion that does not believe in Spirit-filled ministry. They had to spend countless hours seeking God and pursuing His glory.

They had to stand against many who mocked them. They had to give up their reputations and be willing to look foolish in the eyes of the world. This is the price of glory. It is surrender and laying your weaknesses bare.

> And lest I should be exalted above measure by the abundance of revelations, a thorn was given me in the flesh, a messenger of Satan, to torment me, lest I be exalted above measure. I asked the Lord three times that this thing might depart from me. But He said to me, "My grace is sufficient for you, for My strength is made perfect in weakness." Therefore most gladly I will boast in my weaknesses, that the power of Christ may rest upon me. So I take pleasure in weaknesses, in reproaches, in hardships, in persecutions, and in distresses for Christ's sake. For when I am weak, then I am strong.
>
> —2 CORINTHIANS 12:7–10

Paul faced something he described as a thorn in the flesh. A demonic spirit was assigned to harass him everywhere he went to preach because he touched realms of revelation and demonstration that threatened the enemy's kingdom. The enemy was opposing his mind and body in a futile attempt to get him to abandon course, to yield to the pressure.

As he sought God, he was pointed back to grace. God was revealing a paradoxical mystery here. His strength is made perfect in weakness. God's majesty and power are drawn to our weakness. When we are honest, broken, and transparent in the face of Jesus, His glory comes in full force.

Moses had no confidence in his ability to speak, yet God chose him. Paul understood the Hebrews and could easily have spent his entire preaching career ministering to them because it was his culture, yet God chose to send him to a people he did not understand. In weakness these men found God's might. This is one of the mysteries of destiny. God chooses to use unlikely, unqualified people, and He sends them into arenas where they have no ability. Why? Because He wants to receive the glory. He wants us to realize that it is by His power alone and that when we live surrendered, there is absolutely nothing we cannot do.

Our weaknesses make room for His strength! The areas where you lack self-confidence may be the very things heaven breathes upon. He wants to pour out His power and glory in the weak places. In the places you feel you have nothing to offer, God wants to take "the foolish things" and use them "to confound the wise" (1 Cor. 1:27).

> No king is saved by a great army; a mighty man is not delivered by great strength. A horse is a vain hope for safety; it will not deliver by its great strength. The eye of the LORD is on those who fear Him, on those who hope in His lovingkindness, to deliver their soul from death, and to keep alive in famine. Our soul waits for the LORD; He is our help and our shield. For our heart will rejoice in Him, because we have trusted in His holy name. Let Your lovingkindness, O LORD, be on us, just as we hope in You.
>
> —PSALM 33:16–22

We are saved by His power! He is turning our attention and our affection toward Him. He is calling us to move deeper into His majesty. He is speaking destiny and potential over the seemingly insignificant parts of our lives. He is releasing us to world-changing destiny. Just as He came to Moses and breathed on the weak areas of his life, so He is doing in each of us.

PROPHETIC PRAYER

Father, I thank You that where I feel weak, You are strong. I confess Your strength in my life, and I accept Your grace and ability being released into my destiny. I confess that I walk in Your might and power. I confess that You provide answers and solutions. I confess that I move in radical obedience. I decree that Your power and majesty are manifesting in every area of my life, in the name of Jesus. Amen.

MY DECREE OVER YOU

I decree God's glory and power in your life. I see the Lord moving in areas that you feel are broken. I see the majesty of Jesus becoming more real to you as He commissions you for unusual assignments. I decree that He is stretching your yes and revealing Himself *to* you and *through* you in a major way. I bind and break the spirit of fear. God has not given you the spirit of fear but of power, love, and a sound mind, in the name of Jesus. Amen.

POINTS TO CONSIDER

- Have I surrendered every part of my life to God?
- Is there any thread of self or pride left in me?

- Have I been washed in His presence enough to die to my own desires?

- Do I recognize my weaknesses so I can receive His strength?

- Am I so surrendered to Jesus that uncommon power flows through me?

- Have I overcome the fear that has hindered me?

Chapter 13

THE MYSTERY OF TEMPORARY DECREASE

MOSES LEFT THE palace and gave up all the treasures of Egypt to pursue God's plan for his life. This was a temporary decrease that led to a mega increase. Many times we have to surrender our plans or desires for a moment, but it leads to a much higher purpose than we could ever imagine. This is a kingdom mystery. The seed dies, but the resurrection power comes forth!

> By faith Moses, when he became of age, refused to be called the son of Pharaoh's daughter, choosing rather to suffer affliction with the people of God than to enjoy the pleasures of sin for a time. He esteemed the reproach of Christ as greater riches than the treasures in Egypt, for he looked to the reward. By faith he forsook Egypt, not fearing the wrath of the king. He endured by looking to Him who is invisible. By faith he kept the Passover and the sprinkling of blood, lest the one who destroys the firstborn touch them.
>
> By faith they passed through the Red Sea as on dry land, which the Egyptians attempted to do, but were drowned.
>
> —HEBREWS 11:24–29

Moses chose the road of obedience above the road of comfort. This reveals another destiny mystery. The mystery of temporary decrease. Moses planted his life as a seed in the will of God. He was not concerned about the financial or physical sacrifice. He was going for destiny.

This act of obedience is mentioned in God's hall of faith scriptures! God is commending the faith of Moses. Faith always empowers action and obedience. Faith without corresponding action is dead (Jas. 2:17). Your faith will demand a reply. It will demand obedience because miracles are always on the other side of radical obedience.

Moses was destined to lead a move of miracles!

> Then He said: Indeed, I am going to make a covenant before all your people. I will do wonders such as have not been done in all the earth nor in any nation. And all the people among whom you live will see the work of the LORD, for it is a fearful thing that I will do with you.
> —Exodus 34:10

No man or woman can ever truly experience the miracle realm without obedience. Obedience is the result of the voice of the Lord. Once you have heard from heaven, it becomes much easier to take a step of faith. Moses was mantled for the supernatural. God's mandate upon him was one of power and wonders. He was called to represent the kingdom in all its power.

Moses was delivered from fear. You cannot walk in fear and faith at the same time! In fact fear will bring spiritual paralysis. When fear grips, you are unable to advance. Faith is a spirit that advances and moves ahead, seizing the promises and possessing them. It empowers possession in the realm of the spirit. When you walk by faith, you are able to lay hold of the promise.

SURRENDER IN BEING PLANTED

The mystery of planting must be understood. When Moses said yes to the call, part of him came to life, and another part seemed to die. This is the process of planting. No seed can produce fruit without first being planted. When we plant the seed, it may feel like a death. In one way it is, because we are essentially letting go of something. We are releasing what is in our hands in exchange for what is in God's hand. The release of the seed gives permission to heaven to release the promise.

These moments can be scary as our minds struggle to figure out what to do. This is our carnal man attempting to dominate our spirit man. In these moments we are standing in front of a doorway into an increased level of kingdom function. We have a simple choice to make. Will we surrender or not? Will we face our own fears or not? Will we trust the voice of our Father or not?

I vividly remember one such moment in my own life. I was in my late teens and had just experienced a radical conversion in my life. I was a new believer sitting in a church when I heard the voice of the Lord speak to me. He told me He had called me. My first hurdle was getting over my own reasons why God could never call me. Didn't He know how messed up I was? Didn't He realize I already had plans? Surely the Lord knew I didn't have ambitions of ministry.

He patiently answered all my questions one by one. After a considerable struggle I accepted that I had indeed heard from Him and that He had a call for my life. To be perfectly honest, I wasn't at all happy about it, but I chose to obey Him. I began then to seek the pathway for training.

I was called but clueless! It only confirms to me what a good sense of humor the Lord has. Through a process, I heard the leading of the Lord to move across the nation and attend Bible college. This was a death on many levels. I had to leave almost all my family as well as a place and culture I loved and go somewhere by faith with almost no resources. I was putting my agenda to death.

The first few days in my new home proved tremendously challenging on every level. I had no money, and I felt lonely and misunderstood. Though I didn't know it then, God was breaking demonic bondage off my life, one step at a time. My soul was being purged. This was the formation of my globetrotting ministry. Over the next couple years I wanted to quit a thousand times, but each time, I found the Lord and His grace in the midst of my trial.

I look back at it now, and I just thank God. I met my wife and made lifelong friends in Bible college. I was radically delivered and changed there. My personal death became a launchpad for global exploits and more importantly for a personal relationship with the Father.

> I have been crucified with Christ [that is, in Him I have shared His crucifixion]; it is no longer I who live, but Christ lives in me. The life I now live in the body I live by faith [by adhering to, relying on, and completely trusting] in the Son of God, who loved me and gave Himself up for me. I do not ignore or nullify the [gracious gift of the] grace of God [His amazing, unmerited favor], for if righteousness comes through [observing] the Law, then Christ died needlessly. [His suffering and death would have had no purpose whatsoever.]
>
> —GALATIANS 2:20–21, AMP

Paul perfectly describes this beautiful journey of temporary decrease. Our pride, desires, and ambition decrease so that the kingdom may be magnified in us and through us. We are actually increasing in the affirmation of our sonship and identity, even though it may feel like a death in that exact moment. Also, Paul reaffirms the role of grace. When my flesh does not want to surrender, when my natural mind is screaming, there is grace to empower my yes!

Every surrender requires a yes. I find the most exquisite dimensions of His grace when I come to the end of myself. Moses had to come to the end of himself. He had to lay it all on the line and say yes. His yes released grace in his life. It released divine ability and power and brought Him to the majesty of Jesus.

> When God created the first living thing, He gave it the ability to grow and multiply. How? Through the principle of sowing and reaping. Life begins by this principle, and since birth your life has operated by this same principle. Harvest springs from the good or bad seeds you have sown, whether or not you were consciously aware of your seed-planting. The principle continues today. To overcome life's problems, reach your potential in life, see your life become fruitful, multiplied, replenished (that is, in health, finance, spiritual renewal, family—your entire being), determine to follow God's law of seedtime and harvest.[1]
>
> —JACK HAYFORD

We are continually sowing seed and living in a harvest. This can be both positive and negative. For example, if we criticize, slander, and tear down other people, we are sowing toxic seed. If we lift up others, pray for them, and release forgiveness even when they wrong us, we are sowing mercy. We must realize the power of these spiritual laws.

As long as planet Earth exists, the law of seedtime and harvest will be alive. We will continually sow and reap. When we sow or release the seed, it may seem like a decrease, but in reality it is the beginning of a major breakthrough and increase. This is never truer than when it pertains to your spiritual calling and assignment. There will be seasons of releasing certain ambitions and desires. In these seasons it feels as if we are decreasing, but in reality we are being set up to enter new levels of glory and grace.

The principle of the seed is enduring. It is God's law here on earth. Remember our ultimate mandate is to host heaven on earth! We are called to house, steward, and release the kingdom.

> Your kingdom come; Your will be done on earth, as it is in heaven.
>
> —MATTHEW 6:10

The mandate of our lives is to manifest God's kingdom in all its glory. We are born to be kingdom people. We are called to reflect and move in the ways of the kingdom. When people deal with us, they should be seeing and experiencing the kingdom of God.

Sowing and reaping are kingdom laws that govern heaven as well. Our experience with these laws is a manifestation of heaven's protocol. Jesus had to go to the depths of hell (be planted) so that He could resurrect and cause a multiplicity of men and women to come to His saving knowledge of grace and salvation. His destiny was to do the will of the Father.

Jesus decreased temporarily on the cross. The decrease was nothing in comparison to the harvest of souls that would come forth. People are being saved daily because of His one act of obedience. Your yes to a temporary decrease can have results that affect generations.

It is part of the heaven-on-earth mandate. I always think of

God's global plans when I read the Lord's Prayer. I think about God's heart for nations and His promise of the knowledge of the glory sweeping the entire planet. Even though those visions are good, there is a much deeper and more personal application of the Lord's Prayer. "Your kingdom come; Your will be done on earth [on the dust], as it is in heaven" (Matt. 6:10). What are we made of?

> Then the LORD God formed man from the dust of the ground and breathed into his nostrils the breath of life, and man became a living being.
> —GENESIS 2:7

Man was made of the dust of the earth! We are created from the earth to carry the DNA of heaven inside of us, causing it to surge all around us. Heaven should be spilling out everywhere we go—not just in a church service but in the marketplace, in the school systems, in media, in education, in every facet of life where believers are present. This is how the glory will sweep the earth. It must first sweep us!

The glory will empower a difficult yes because we understand that our time, our money, our words, our actions—our very lives—are seeds. We are seed bearers, and we can plant with a high expectation of harvest.

> A generation comes, and a generation goes, but the earth continually remains.
> —ECCLESIASTES 1:4

Generations come and go, but the laws of the spirit remain. Seeds will be sown, and harvests will come. We believe these words, but what if we lived with this mindset? What if we became so intentional about surrender and sowing that we lived daily with this in mind? I believe it would release us into a dimension of explosive results and breakthrough.

The kingdom is in many ways a backward kingdom.

> So the last will be first, and the first last. For many are called, but few are chosen.
>
> —MATTHEW 20:16

The first shall be last and the last first. God's order is not like that of man. God's wisdom and ways are not like ours. We might experience something that seems like a setback, when in reality it is a setup. The Bible tells us that we must first sow before reaping. We must release something sacrificial and perhaps even painful to experience a bountiful harvest. If we are being led by human wisdom, we will never do it! When we die to our own lives, we find His life. We are instructed to humble ourselves, and then God will exalt us. All these kingdom laws contradict the ways of man. That is why we must be God seekers. We need His wisdom and revelation to fulfill our appointed destiny.

We must discern the mystery of temporary decrease. Jochebed birthed Moses, and he laid it all on the line to do what God called him to do. He let go of protection and prestige. He planted his life and was raised up in glory. This is a prophetic application for us. When we are planted, the glory is released. As we embrace the planting process, we set ourselves up for a harvest of kingdom glory, power, and service. We fulfill the Lord's Prayer of heaven on earth through our daily lives. Let your yes be a catalyst for the kingdom to rule in you and through you.

PROPHETIC PRAYER

Lord, I thank You for seedtime and harvest. I live as a seed planted in Your kingdom. I decree that I am obedient. I decree that I hear Your voice, discern Your leading, and embrace the process of growth. Help me to increase my level of surrender, Lord. Help me to be faithful and obedient to all that You have called me to do. Help me to host Your glory in my life. Let Your kingdom come in me and through me. Let Your will be done in every area of my life, in the name of Jesus. Amen.

MY DECREE OVER YOU

I decree heaven on earth in your life. I decree miraculous harvest in your life. I decree breakthrough and power. I declare that you are obedient to the voice of God and quick to follow His prompting. I see you moving in greater glory. I see you breaking out and breaking forth. I call forth a breakthrough anointing in your life. I call forth breakthrough power in your life. I bind up every spirit of doubt and unbelief, and I say that you walk by faith and not by sight. You are bold. You are fearless. You love the glory, and you are quick to respond when heaven speaks, in the name of Jesus. Amen.

POINTS TO CONSIDER

- Have I sincerely left my plans behind and sought God's plans for me?

- Has my faith annihilated fear and eliminated spiritual paralysis?

- Have I grown and stretched my faith so that I possess the promises of God?

- Have I decreased so that He may be increased in me?

- Have I surrendered my plans and agendas to adopt His?

- Am I reflecting the kingdom in all my dealings with others?

- Do I sow seeds of mercy and grace or toxic seeds?

- Am I really a God seeker? Do I follow His ways?

Chapter 14

THE MYSTERY OF FIRE

EVERY DELIVERER WILL first pass through fire. The presence of fire is the validation of a calling. Fire is uncomfortable and creates a sensation of death, but it burns away that which potentially withholds the power and glory of God. Through the fire God reconfirmed the call of Moses and fulfilled the prayers of Jochebed. Every deliverer will pass through four types of fire, and we will discuss them in this chapter. Not understanding these fires can cause a person to misread what is taking place in his or her life.

Deliverers are called to bring the forth the fire of God and to destroy the powers of hell! Deliverance sets fire to the works of the enemy. John the Baptist was one of the most significant prophets in the Bible; some even say he was *the* most significant. Think about that for a moment. We find no record of John making any type of prophetic prediction, yet Jesus refers to him as a great prophet!

> Truly I say to you, among those who are born of women, there has risen no one greater than John the Baptist. But he who is least in the kingdom of heaven is greater than he. From the days of John the Baptist until now, the kingdom of heaven has forcefully advanced, and

the strong take it by force. For all the Prophets and
the Law prophesied until John.

—MATTHEW 11:11–13

John held a unique place in history. He announced the Lord
Jesus and prophesied the beginning of the new covenant. John
bridged the gap between old and new. In the verses in Matthew
11 Jesus was not commending John's personal talent or ability
but his role in the transition of history and his announcement
of Jesus.

As a prophet, John called the people of God to repentance
and prepared the way of the Lord. He ushered in a new era as
Jesus emerged on the scene, manifesting the kingdom of God
and preparing for the crucifixion.

> In those days John the Baptist came, preaching in
> the wilderness of Judea, and saying, "Repent, for the
> kingdom of heaven is at hand." For this is he who was
> spoken of by the prophet Isaiah, saying: "The voice of
> one crying in the wilderness: 'Prepare the way of the
> Lord; make His paths straight.'"
>
> This same John had clothing made of camel's hair, a
> leather belt around his waist, and his food was locusts
> and wild honey. Then Jerusalem, and all Judea, and all
> the region around the Jordan went out to him, and were
> baptized by him in the Jordan, confessing their sins.
>
> —MATTHEW 3:1–6

John lived a rugged life and delivered a bold message. He
called out the sins of men and urged them to repent, baptizing
people in the Jordan River. This was the work of preparation for
the crucifixion of the Lord of glory.

John was not prim or proper. He was not a product of the
religious system of the day. He was a wilderness prophet with

off-the-charts boldness and a radical fire. His food was as wild as his unparalleled passion. He was not polished, but he was mantled in the secret place to announce the Lord.

John also carried the fire of God. He was raised up by God to mark the end of a law-giving system of religion. The law only taught men and women how lost and broken they were. Nobody could adequately fulfill the law, which is why grace was imperative. John was used by God to lay the ax to the root of that old system and to prepare the hearts of men for a new system.

The role of prophets is to announce new things, to shake things up, to say the difficult things. Prophets do not look for popularity but are intent upon pleasing the Lord and stewarding His glory. They are called to announce Him and turn the hearts of men and women toward Him.

For this reason prophets are often reviled and misunderstood, but they find their joy in pleasing the Lord and Him alone. Seasoned prophets have thick skin and can endure the weaponry of hell. They must, especially since they are called to be spiritual warriors.

> But when he saw many of the Pharisees and Sadducees come to his baptism, he said to them, "O generation of vipers, who has warned you to escape from the wrath to come? Therefore, bear fruit worthy of repentance, and do not think to say within yourselves, 'We have Abraham as our father,' for I say to you that God is able from these stones to raise up children for Abraham. Even now the axe is put to the tree roots. Therefore, every tree which does not bear good fruit is cut down and thrown into the fire.
>
> "I indeed baptize you with water to repentance, but He who is coming after me is mightier than I, whose

shoes I am not worthy to carry. He will baptize you
with the Holy Spirit and with fire. His fan is in His
hand, and He will thoroughly clean His floor and
gather His wheat into the granary, but He will burn
up the chaff with unquenchable fire."

—MATTHEW 3:7–12

John boldly rebuked the guardians of the old system! This was
part of his prophetic DNA. He was called to reveal Jesus and
to announce His arrival. He was used to herald the changing of
covenants and eras! He was testifying of the lordship of Jesus.

John announced the baptism of fire. He announced the
coming work of Jesus and Holy Spirit, as the fire of God would
set a generation ablaze and launch the ekklesia as a force in the
earth. John knew and understood God's fire. He was a deliverer;
every deliverer will pass through fire. It is a requirement of the
calling. You must have the fire of God in your life.

Moses knew the fire of God. He was called to bring
deliverance to a nation and a generation. He had grown weary
on the backside of the wilderness when God's power showed up
in the midst of a fire. Deliverers are announced in the presence
of fire.

The fire of God will both purge and accelerate your life. In
fact you will find fresh dimensions of God in the midst of fire.
Fire is a choice instrument in preparation for your destiny.

For our God is a consuming fire.

—HEBREWS 12:29

God is a consuming fire! The presence of God sets people
ablaze, spiritually speaking. They do not just encounter fire or
see fire; they are drawn into the fire and are consumed. Another

way to look at this is to become swallowed up. Imagine your life becoming totally surrounded and engulfed by the fire of God.

What would happen? Your thinking would change. Your mode of operation would change. Your passion would change. This is the mission of God's fire in your life. It is sent as fuel for complete transformation.

I will never forget one of my early encounters with the fire of God. I was young and newly saved. God was purging sin and brokenness out of my life. I spent hours of "carpet time" (lying alone, face on the floor) crying out to God. The more I sought Him, the stronger my hunger grew. The only thing that could satisfy my quest was the presence of God.

I went to church one morning, and the spirit of prophecy came upon me. I could feel God's power bubbling up from my belly, and I was trying my best to push it back down! I was embarrassed and didn't know anything about prophetic ministry, but I had been praying with a small, fired-up prayer group in the church, and they had been encouraging me in the prophetic.

I told the Lord that I would only move in the gift if He made it very plain! This is not a good idea because we are to be led by the Spirit of God, not external things. These outward things can confirm, and I believe in signs, but the primary leading is found in your spirit man. Also, in public prophetic ministry, you have to follow the order of the place that you are in and obey authority.

> Let every person be subject to the governing authorities,
> for there is no authority except from God, and those
> that exist are appointed by God.
> —Romans 13:1

After I prayed my silly prayer, the pastor said he felt someone had a prophetic word. I looked around, and no one moved. This was my sign! I was still scared and did not budge. Man of faith that I was, I told God to please do something else and make it even more obvious! The pastor made another appeal, this time disclosing that the person with the word had never prophesied. He described how nervous the person was and described my internal battle to a tee. Finally, I responded, trembling and afraid, but doing my best to obey God.

He invited me to the front. I closed my eyes and began to prophesy. I couldn't tell you what came out of my mouth that day. It gushed forth out of my belly like a river. God was training me in public prophetic ministry. When I opened my eyes, people were kneeling, bowing, trembling, and crying all over the sanctuary. Some were still standing, but God's fire had obviously hit that place the same way it had hit my belly. That was the beginning of a ministry marked by fire. I was launched in the fire.

Four Types of Fire

Deliverance demands fire. Your life needs the fire of God. The formation of your destiny requires several types of fire.

1. Fiery trials

> Beloved, think it not strange concerning the fiery trial which is to try you, as though some strange thing happened unto you: but rejoice, inasmuch as ye are partakers of Christ's sufferings; that, when his glory shall be revealed, ye may be glad also with exceeding joy.
>
> —1 Peter 4:12–13, kjv

You will pass through fiery trials if you are a deliverer. The enemy shows up to inspect your faith and test your resolve. He shakes everything he can shake to see if you will move. This is an age-old process, but the power of God can cause you to stand.

Rejoice when resistance comes. I tell people to let their warfare be the confirmation. Instead of giving way to doom and gloom, rejoice. If the enemy were not threatened by you, he would not be fighting you. Every calling demands tenacity. With God's grace and power, you must resist the enemy and press through. The Bible says the Lord is our help in troubled times.

> God is our refuge and strength, a well-proven help in trouble. Therefore we will not fear, though the earth be removed, and though the mountains be carried into the midst of the sea; though its waters roar and foam, though the mountains shake with its swelling. Selah
>
> There is a river whose streams make glad the city of God, the holy dwelling place of the Most High. God is in the midst of her; she will not be moved; God will help her in the early dawn.
>
> —Psalm 46:1–5

The power of God will protect and preserve you! He will keep you from getting moved from the promise of heaven if you choose to praise and magnify Him no matter what hell says. When fiery trials come to you, God has Holy Ghost power to sustain you. If you praise your way through and refuse to give up, you will come out on the other side with power and authority you did not have before.

2. Refiner's fire

> And I will bring the third part through the fire, and
> will refine them as silver is refined, and will try them
> as gold is tried: they shall call on my name, and I will
> hear them: I will say, It is my people: and they shall say,
> The LORD is my God.
>
> —ZECHARIAH 13:9, KJV

God's fire refines you. It burns away the impurities. This
is one of the richest blessings in life, to pass through the
purification of fire. Your flesh will burn and sizzle, but it is
necessary to get where God is taking you. When you pray for
fire, a cleansing shows up.

Deliverers must be freed from insecurities, ambition, and
pride. The refiner's fire will accomplish this. Peter had denied
knowing Jesus three times, but after the fire of God hit in the
Upper Room, Peter was delivered from fear and preached Jesus
to the masses. Refiner's fire will totally transform you.

3. Fire and glory

> Moses went up to the mountain, and the cloud covered
> the mountain. The glory of the LORD rested on Mount
> Sinai, and the cloud covered it for six days. And on the
> seventh day He called to Moses from the midst of the
> cloud. Now the appearance of the glory of the LORD
> was like a consuming fire on the top of the mountain
> to the eyes of the children of Israel. Moses went into
> the midst of the cloud and went up to the mountain.
> And Moses was on the mountain for forty days and
> forty nights.
>
> —EXODUS 24:15–18

This is one of the most brilliant types of fire. God's fire and glory come to encounter, to abide, and to draw deliverers deeper into all that He has. It is an abiding fire, a fire that draws you to the person of Jesus in all His glory.

For forty days Moses was caught up in the brilliance of Yahweh. There is no account of him eating or drinking. The fire and the glory overrode natural laws and provided limitless possibilities.

I believe that God wants to commission a generation in His fire and glory. There is a sending aspect to the fire and glory. When men and women have been mantled in the fire and glory, they carry an unstoppable tenacity. May we see God's fire and glory in our midst in a way that forever transforms us.

4. Prophetic fire

> But if I say, "I will not make mention of Him nor speak any more in His name," then His word was in my heart as a burning fire shut up in my bones; and I was weary of forbearing it, and I could not endure it.
> —JEREMIAH 20:9

Jeremiah's words demonstrate the power of a fiery prophetic anointing. If you try to shut down the word of the Lord in a prophet or a prophetic person, it becomes like a shut-up fire. They have to release it. Burning words are in the bellies of prophetic men and women all over the earth.

Jeremiah may have tried to walk away from his prophetic mandate, but he could not. Something was burning in his belly. Something was stirring, and it was too much to contain. He could not quench the eruptive, prophetic fire.

May God raise up a generation of prophets and prophetic people who steward the revelation of God's word with boldness, sincerity, and integrity. May they set regions and nations ablaze!

When we think about Moses' encounter of fire at the burning bush, we get excited. We find ourselves praying and asking God for such a sign. One day I was pondering this very thing, and the Lord began to speak to me.

He told me many are praying to *see* a burning bush, but He desires that they *become* a burning bush. Moses was an Old Testament saint who lived in a different covenant. At that time, God was on the outside of men and women working with external circumstances to lead and guide them. Jesus came so that God could live in the hearts of men and women.

> I urge you therefore, brothers, by the mercies of God, that you present your bodies as a living sacrifice, holy, and acceptable to God, which is your reasonable service of worship.
>
> —Romans 12:1

We are urged to offer our bodies as a living sacrifice. We are called to place ourselves in the midst of the fire. We should have the fire in us, upon us, and emanating from us. This is the baptism of fire that John prophesied about. It is not just an external encounter. It is a full submersion.

The burning bush hosted the voice of the Lord. God spoke through a blazing tree. I believe Jesus wants us to become living, breathing, burning trees hosting the fire of His presence. Our lives are to host His flame so that His voice can be heard loudly and clearly through us.

This is the mystery of fire. God's fire is formed in us to release Jesus through us. We may be going through uncomfortable burning, we may be experiencing fiery trials, but it is all leading us to deeper purpose and surrender. We must become acquainted with the fire. Champions are formed in the fire!

PROPHETIC PRAYER

Father, I thank You for Your radical, cleansing fire in my life. I submit to Your fire. I claim the fire of deliverance in my life. I claim the fire of revival in my life. I claim Your cleansing fire in my life. Thank You that I am a fire carrier and Your glory emanates from my life. Thank You that I have Your fire in every area of my life, in the name of Jesus. Amen.

MY DECREE OVER YOU

I decree holy fire in your life. I call forth strength and stamina that you come through the cleansing fire and fiery trials. I say that you will not quit. You will not back down, and you will not be defeated. I decree God's fire upon you to release His boldness. I decree that your life is a platform for His fire and His voice to speak to others. I decree the baptism of fire in your life, in the mighty name of Jesus. Amen.

POINTS TO CONSIDER

- Do I live Romans 12:1 as a living sacrifice for my Lord?
- Have I laid down myself, my ambitions, my dreams for His?
- Has Christ been formed in me, or do I still have excuses?

- Do I murmur and complain, or am I a voice of God?

- Have I allowed the fire of God to refine me?

- Am I a casual Christian or a burning bush?

- Has my destiny been formed and validated in the fire?

- Am I committed to praising and magnifying Him even in the midst of trials?

Chapter 15

THE MYSTERY OF
PERSONAL AWAKENING

A T THE BURNING bush, dormant plans and purposes were awakened in the heart of Moses. These were the very things for which Jochebed had fought. Many times we go through a desert season and feel as though we have lost our vision for the radical call on our lives. In moments of personal awakening we are restored back to proper vision and mission.

We often become shallow believers who are moved by our own human circumstances. While I understand that we are human beings with thoughts, feelings, and experiences, I also know that we must live lives built on the eternal and not on the temporary.

> We have the same spirit of faith. As it is written, "I believed, and therefore I have spoken." So we also believe and therefore speak, knowing that He who raised the Lord Jesus will also raise us through Jesus and will present us with you. All these things are for your sakes, so that the abundant grace through the thanksgiving of many might overflow to the glory of God.
>
> For this reason we do not lose heart: Even though our outward man is perishing, yet our inward man is being renewed day by day. Our light affliction, which

lasts but for a moment, works for us a far more exceeding and eternal weight of glory, while we do not look at the things which are seen, but at the things which are not seen. For the things which are seen are temporal, but the things which are not seen are eternal.

—2 CORINTHIANS 4:13–18

The spirit of faith empowers us to see far beyond temporary shaking and turbulence. We choose to rise above the things we feel, see, and hear to stand boldly and unashamedly upon the Word of God.

As we walk by faith, we speak the Word of God. We speak what heaven says about us, our families, our calling, and our lives. We do not give place to the enemy by murmuring and complaining, even though our flesh may want to at any given moment.

MAKING AN ETERNAL IMPACT

At the end of these verses we are given a key. Paul instructs the church at Corinth to look at the things which are eternal and not temporary. Think about the simple yet profound truth revealed in this statement. Isn't this the whole point of the journey? Aren't we supposed to live as disciples of Christ, as people who are *in* this world but not *of* it? Isn't this the real intended focus of our lives?

What would our lives look like if we woke up daily evaluating our imprint on eternity? Instead of focusing on the right job, car, or opportunity (all of which can be important in the affairs of life and family), what would happen if we blocked everything out by returning back to that which is eternal?

How did this apply to Moses at the burning bush? He had settled for a "normal" life far outside the real mission God had given him as a deliverer. Jochebed did not hide him and put him in the river to fulfill the role of a wanderer. She had prayed, heard from God, and put him in the river at exactly the right time. Favor manifested, and he came to live in the house of Pharaoh. This was a complete and absolute turnaround. He went from being hunted by the palace to being protected by the same people! Don't tell me that God is not mighty.

> Then his sister said to Pharaoh's daughter, "Shall I go and call for you a nursing woman of the Hebrew women so that she may nurse the child for you?"
>
> And Pharaoh's daughter said to her, "Go." So the young girl went and called the child's mother. Pharaoh's daughter said to her, "Take this child away, and nurse him for me, and I will give you your wages." So the woman took the child and nursed him. Now the child grew, and she brought him to Pharaoh's daughter, and he became her son. And she called his name Moses and said, "Because I drew him out of the water."
>
> —Exodus 2:7–10

God set up the whole thing. Jochebed released Moses into the river as a seed. God led her to give up her precious child. Only God could have orchestrated it so perfectly that everything would line up at the right time. Jochebed then became Moses' nanny. She was given the gift of being in the life of her son and tending to him as a mother would her infant.

She made these sacrifices in light of God's call upon Moses' life. The Jochebed anointing will take bold, radical steps to obey God. The Jochebed anointing is prophetic, moving under the direction of the voice of God. The Jochebed anointing ushers in the glory that births deliverance and deliverers.

Moses was called to a people and a nation, but he ended

up away from his place of assignment. He needed a personal awakening. When life pounds us and the enemy wages against us, it is easy to lose our focus. We can become like Moses, isolated and confused, wandering in the desolate places.

What happened to turn the spiritual tide in the life of Moses? A fire, glory, and the voice of the Lord showed up. Moses had a personal awakening. He was awakened to the plans of God, to spiritual hunger, and to the prophetic voice of God.

Oh, how we need personal awakening! It is not good enough for God to touch everyone around us. We need the touch of God in our own lives. We need to be hungry and thirsty for the living God. We need fresh impartation and vision for our lives. We need the anointing flowing like a river to destroy all the yokes the lying devil has put upon us.

ANOINTING OUR EYES

> I counsel you to buy from Me gold refined by fire, that you may be rich, and white garments, that you may be dressed, that the shame of your nakedness may not appear, and anoint your eyes with eye salve, that you may see.
>
> —REVELATION 3:18

We need a fresh anointing upon our eyes. When our eyes are anointed with fresh oil, we can clearly see the purposes and the mandate of God for our life. In the Book of Revelation the Lord Jesus is instructing a satisfied and complacent people to anoint their eyes. Like Samuel in the Old Testament, the church of Laodicea had lost its sight.

If the enemy can rob you of your vision, he can defeat you. He wants to mute your spiritual eyesight and diminish your passion for seeing in the spirit. He wants you to stumble around in the dark because demons hide under cover of darkness.

Personal awakening will revive your prophetic sight and cause dreams and visions to surge in your life as God begins to reveal your mission and your future.

During my Bible college years as a young man, I had an awesome encounter with God. Suddenly I was swept up into the glory realm, and Jesus began to speak to me. He spoke to me about my purpose and mandate. He spoke to me about the mission of my life. He spoke to me about the power of His Spirit.

In the midst of this encounter my spiritual eyes began to see. I saw the future. I saw my life and what God intended for me to build over my lifetime. That vision framed my entire ministry. I am still partnering with heaven to execute those ordained plans.

I don't wake up in the morning trying to find a sense of purpose. I wake up filled with opportunity and priorities as I live out the vision that Jesus gave me for my life. Backslidden and oppressed people have forgotten the vision for their lives! They have returned to the very things that God brought them out of. This is the result of a vacancy of spiritual vision. Spiritually blind people don't know where they are going.

> But it has happened to them according to the true proverb, "The dog returns to his own vomit," and "the sow that was washed to her wallowing in the mud."
> —2 Peter 2:22

This verse is speaking of false teachers and deceptive ministers, but it applies to the backslidden as well. Hell's mission is to quench the vision of God in the lives of people, to cause them to return to the very things from which Jesus has delivered them. In fact this is always the aim of spiritual attacks: to restore bondage that has been broken. Hell comes to make the people of God give up! This is why we cannot afford to live with a spirit of slumber. We need to be active and alert in the spirit realm. We need personal awakening.

> Be sober and watchful, because your adversary the devil walks around as a roaring lion, seeking whom he may devour.
>
> —1 Peter 5:8

Intimacy Produces Awakening

I remember several years ago I was part of a spontaneous and phenomenal move of God. Jesus saved, healed, and delivered many. He was truly lighting a spiritual fire in a region, and it was glorious to be a part of it. I would have gone and just supported the meetings, but I had the privilege of being right in the middle of what God was doing.

During this time, I discovered a secret. I found that the more I experienced Jesus, the more I craved His presence. I would tell people the key to revival and awakening. We often pray for nations, churches, and people. We cry aloud, asking God to send awakening and revival. Meanwhile our own vision and passion are dim.

During those meetings, I used to draw a circle around myself with my finger and say, "Revival begins here!" I would tell the Lord that I wanted to be a burning one. I wanted awakening in my life!

Night after night in those meetings as I ministered, I would lean into the Lord. I would search His heart and His agenda, not just for the people but also for me! I would often find myself face down on the floor, crying out to Jesus. Awakening is a personal mandate! Each of us must desire the heart of the Lord manifesting daily in the simplest parts of our lives.

What would awakening look like in your family? What if you began hosting the kingdom on the job or in the marketplace? How would your relationships and activities be affected by a greater awareness of the presence of Jesus and His plan for your life?

God called Moses back to purpose and urged him back to His plans and intent. By awakening Moses, God broke through his hard heart, his wounds, his frustration, and his fear. Moses had a list of excuses, but God's blazing glory burned through each one. I believe He wants to do the same thing now in your life.

He wants to release personal awakening. He wants to blaze through every fear and stoke the fires of eternal destiny in you. He wants to breathe upon old visions and hidden purpose. He wants to restore a first-love lifestyle.

> Also I heard the voice of the Lord saying, "Whom shall I send, and who will go for us?"
> Then I said, "Here am I. Send me."
>
> —ISAIAH 6:8

During Isaiah's dramatic encounter with the Lord, he prayed, "Here am I, Lord. Send me!" This prayer becomes a catalyst for personal awakening. Ask the Father to send you where you need to go. One of my favorite prayers is claiming ordained steps. I thank the Lord that He has ordered my steps, and I pray that He directs me. He can send me where He sees fit. This is a prayer that opens the door for personal awakening.

Allow God to breathe on you and reveal where you need to be, who you need to do life with, and what His mission is for you. Lay down your preconceived ideas at the feet of Jesus. Hunger, passion, fervent prayer, obedience, surrender, and prophetic insight are all ingredients of awakening.

PROPHETIC PRAYER

Lord, I thank You for anointing my eyes with Your eye salve. Thank You for restoring my vision. Thank You that I see Your beauty and majesty. Thank You for awakening in my life, Lord. Awaken the parts of me that need to be awakened. I surrender to You and Your plans for my life. I want to live in Your purpose for my life. I want to live fully surrendered to You and in the midst of Your move. I thank You for the right people, the right plans, and the right timing for my destiny, in the name of Jesus. Amen.

MY DECREE OVER YOU

I decree the fire of revival and awakening in your life. I decree God's cleansing fire. I decree God's glory over you and around you. I decree revelation and insight. I release a fresh anointing over your eyes and command all hardness of heart to be removed. I command your heart to line up with the plans of the Father, in the name of Jesus. Amen.

POINTS TO CONSIDER

- ✎ Do I seek the heart of God to know His plans for my life each day?
- ✎ Am I hungry for personal awakening, personal revival?

- Do I just go about life without zeal or fire?

- Do I become depressed when under attack?

- Do I entertain thoughts of my old life when trials come?

- Have I allowed God to blaze through my fears?

- Do I stoke the fires of eternal destiny in my life?

- Am I truly hungry for more of Him?

Chapter 16

THE MYSTERY OF FREEDOM IN THE GLORY

Moses could not go forth without freedom. Jochebed's prayers and intercession had secured his freedom. In the glory God brought power and deliverance to Moses. We often think about the glory of God as an experience, but it is much more than that. The glory is the evidence of the King, it is the up-close presence of God, it is the full weight of His kingdom, and it is the brilliance of His majesty. We can learn to fight and overcome in the glory dimension. This is a key prophetic truth for intercessors and warriors. It is the mystery of freedom in the glory. The presence of the glory of God is the evidence that the King is in the room. If the King is present, then freedom is present. In fact Jesus and bondage do not mix!

> All Your works shall praise You, O Lord, and Your godly ones shall bless You. They shall speak of the glory of Your kingdom and talk of Your power, to make known to people His mighty acts, and the glorious majesty of His kingdom. Your kingdom is an everlasting kingdom, and Your dominion endures throughout all generations.
>
> —Psalm 145:10–13

The glory is connected to the kingdom! You cannot experience the glory of God without the works of His kingdom. When authentic glory shows up, the power and majesty of Jesus enters the atmosphere. As His power and majesty enter, demonic entities begin to manifest.

I have seen this time and again while ministering. The glory of God will come into a meeting, and suddenly demons will act out. They become stirred by the presence of a higher authority. When the glory comes into a place, it is the weight of God, and it begins to crush demonic beings.

> The God of peace will soon crush Satan under your feet. The grace of our Lord Jesus Christ be with you.
> —ROMANS 16:20

Paul was writing to the Roman church declaring that God would crush Satan under His feet. This was a decree of power and authority. Jesus enforces His dominion over the enemy. He has empowered us to act as authorized agents of dominion and power over the works of hell. When glory shows up, deliverance bursts forth like a supernatural gushing. This is the fruit of the kingdom.

EMBRACING THE GLORY

> The voice of the LORD is over the waters; the God of glory thunders; the LORD is over many waters. The voice of the LORD sounds with strength; the voice of the LORD—with majesty.
> —PSALM 29:3–4

The voice of the Lord releases the strength of the Lord. As His voice thunders, His authoritative decree resounds. His voice carries His glory, which brings forth freedom and deliverance.

189

When we host His voice, we are hosting the announcement of His freedom.

I believe this is one of the reasons the enemy hates prophets and prophetic people. When they speak of the glorious One and announce His plans, it brings confusion to the camp of the enemy. The enemy hates prophetic churches and gatherings because they will expose his hidden schemes.

God's radiant glory shines brightly in the midst of dark places. God's glory brings illumination, insight, and strength. You are strengthened in the glory realm.

> It is evident that God is in the business of forgiving, exalting cities, healing lands, and giving the nations and the uttermost parts of the earth as an inheritance. To see His Kingdom manifested and His glory in the lands in which we are positioned, oftentimes it will involve an engagement in prophetic intercession, prophetic decrees, and strategic warfare prayer.[1]
>
> —Rebecca Greenwood

God's answer to cities, regions, and nations in need of awakening and freedom is the manifest presence of God. When the King comes in, freedom is manifested and revival bursts forth. What would it look like if we changed our thought processes about glory and began to realize that we can fight, win, and prevail in the midst of the glory of God? What if we believed that the glory of God empowers us for unprecedented freedom?

Moses was sent forth with a glory mandate to manifest the full weight of the kingdom of God. He was given two prophets to speak the word of the Lord. Glory will always unveil the voice and revelation of the Lord. His voice is housed in glory. When the Old Testament prophets saw Him and heard His voice, they encountered His glory.

Above the expanse that was over their heads was the
likeness of a throne, as the appearance of a sapphire
stone. And on the likeness of the throne was the
likeness as the appearance of a man on it high up.
Then I saw as glowing metal, as the appearance of fire
all around within it, from the appearance of His loins
and upward; and from the appearance of His loins and
downward I saw as it were the appearance of fire, and
there was a brightness around Him. As the appearance
of the rainbow that is in the cloud on a day of rain, so
was the appearance of the brightness all around.

This was the appearance of the likeness of the glory
of the LORD. And when I saw it, I fell on my face and
heard a voice of one speaking.

—EZEKIEL 1:26–28

Ezekiel was taken into the throne room. He saw the four
living creatures, the brilliance of God, and the fire of His
presence. The glory caused Ezekiel to fall on his face. The
weight of God's presence brought Ezekiel low. This is the typical
response to the glory of God.

When heavy glory shows up, the ways of man must bow low.
Fleshly concerns bow before the glory. When the glory of God
shows up, demonic systems are crushed! When the glory of
God shows up, the awe of God is present. Prophets love the
glory of God.

A throne represents dominion. The throne of a king is a
manifestation of his glory. The throne is the place where the
monarch sits and where the government is represented. It is
impossible to dissociate the glory of God with the government
of God. When we host His glory, we are also hosting His government and invited into His freedom! There is a realm of win-
ning and getting set free in the glory!

DIMENSIONS OF FREEDOM IN THE GLORY

The up-close expression of Jesus

The glory of God is a proximity anointing. When glory shows up, you are up close to the person of Jesus! Glory is atmospheric.

Brilliance and majesty

The glory manifests the brilliance of Jesus. Out of His brilliance and beauty come revelation and strength. Many times fresh strategies will emerge from the glory of God. The glory of God will bring forth His light and power. The glory of God will open up prophetic insight and wisdom. Glory can help provide insight into critical warfare strategies.

Throne room atmosphere

As we have discussed, the throne room is filled with the glory! When the throne room is present, the governing force of heaven is present, enforcing salvation, healing, miracles, deliverance, and victory!

Bondage-breaking force

Under the weight of His glory, bondage is broken! The glory of God brings people into freedom.

Fire and glory

Fresh fire to burn away bondage, weights, and hindrances comes in the glory of God. There is fire for both personal and corporate deliverance in the glory realm. When the glory of God is moving, there is also a powerful move of deliverance.

Weight and presence

The weight of heaven comes, and unusual things happen. It can scare people who are not knowledgeable about the glory realm, because the glory realm causes strange things to happen. When heaven's weight rests upon a person or people, anything can happen! The weighty glory comes to add influence, favor, value, and abundance. The weighty glory comes to bring the flesh low and lift Jesus high. The weighty glory comes to bring men and women to new levels of encounter and presence.

Bodies will fall under the weight of God's glory. Broken systems and structures will buckle under the weight of God's glory and power. Religious strongholds will be confronted and crushed under the weight of God's glory.

People often pray for revival and encounter, but they are a part of a broken religious system. When the King shows up, His glory will actually crush what they have built because it is fleshly and not spiritual. This is why God gives new wineskins and methods to properly host the glory of God. God reveals plans and structures to host His glory.

> And the priests were not able to stand in order to serve because of the cloud, for the glory of the LORD had filled the house of God.
>
> —2 CHRONICLES 5:14

Silver, gold, and glory

There is financial provision in the glory of God. When the children of Israel came out of bondage, they were loaded down with silver and gold! They were loaded down with wealth and abundance. The glory will cause increase to come to your life.

> And I will shake all nations, and the desire of all nations shall come: and I will fill this house with glory, saith the LORD of hosts. The silver is mine, and the gold is mine, saith the LORD of hosts. The glory of this latter house shall be greater than of the former, saith the LORD of hosts: and in this place will I give peace, saith the LORD of hosts.
>
> —HAGGAI 2:7–9, KJV

Healing, wonders, and glory

Miracles happen in the glory realm. When God delivered His people from Egypt, they came out with strength, wealth, and power. I believe that the glory of God brought healing and strength in their midst. Psalm 105:37 says, "He brought them forth also with silver and gold: and there was not one feeble person among their tribes" (KJV). This was a manifestation of the glory realm. There is a healing dimension of the glory of God.

> Jesus departed from there, and passed by the Sea of Galilee, and went up on a mountain and sat down there. Great crowds came to Him, having with them those who were lame, blind, mute, maimed, and many others, and placed them down at Jesus' feet, and He healed them, so that the crowds wondered when they saw the mute speak, the maimed made whole, the lame walk, and the blind see. And they glorified the God of Israel.
>
> —MATTHEW 15:29–31

Jesus was the embodiment of the kingdom of God. He was the manifestation of the light and brilliance of heaven. Everywhere He went, bondage was confronted, and diseases departed! He carried the full weight of God's glory. Jesus' agenda was to do the will of the Father. His healing ministry pointed people back to the Father. As they entered the glory, they then gave God glory! This caused a glory tsunami. It is a manifestation of His freedom in the glory.

The church is called to be the eyes, ears, hands, and feet of Jesus today. We should be manifesting the same type of glory in our gatherings—people being healed, demons coming out, the prophetic flowing, and miracles happening. If there is no glory, there is no breakthrough. We need to get back to the glory.

And Moses answered and said, "But they will not believe me, nor listen to my voice. For they will say, 'The Lord has not appeared to you.'"

The Lord said to him, "What is that in your hand?"

And he said, "A rod."

He said, "Throw it on the ground."

And he threw it on the ground, and it became a serpent. Then Moses fled from it.

Then the Lord said to Moses, "Put forth your hand and take it by the tail." And he put forth his hand, and caught it, and it became a rod in his hand.

"This is so that they may believe that the Lord, the God of their fathers, the God of Abraham, the God of Isaac, and the God of Jacob, has appeared to you."

The Lord said furthermore to him, "Now put your hand into your bosom." He put his hand into his bosom, and when he took it out, his hand was as leprous as snow.

He said, "Put your hand into your bosom again." So he put his hand into his bosom again and brought it out of his bosom, and it was restored like his other flesh.

"If they will not believe you, nor listen to the voice of the first sign, then they may believe the voice of the latter sign. But if they will not believe also these two signs or listen to your voice, then you shall take water from the river and pour it on the dry land, and the water which you take out of the river will become blood on the dry land."

—Exodus 4:1–9

God gave Moses a ministry of signs and wonders. This is a very misunderstood ministry. God can do strange and unusual things in the natural realm. The signs never show up to get us enamored with them! The signs are intended to point to Jesus.

In the case of Moses the signs were to back up his mandate and message of deliverance.

Signs and wonders happen in the glory realm. You cannot enter into the glory realm and put God in a box! The mandate of freedom—for your life, for cities, and for nations—causes unusual things to happen.

I was preaching in a hotel once and talking about the fire of God. I announced that the fire was coming to my nation and to the people of God. All of a sudden, the fire alarm in the building went off! It kept going off for some time. The staff told us they had no idea what was going on. There was no natural fire. We knew what was going on! This was a confirmation of the message.

Take God out of the box that you have put Him in! He is the Creator of everything. When His freedom and glory show up, mind-blowing miracles, prophetic ministry, and signs and wonders are going to take place. Yield to the glory. You do not have to understand everything. You do not have to have an explanation for everything. You must simply trust God.

I have seen in the spirit a move of greater glory coming. I have seen a move of freedom in the glory coming. The Jochebed anointing is a glory anointing. For a generation of kingdom deliverers to arise, we must learn to walk in the glory, move in the glory, fight from the glory, and prevail with the glory.

When God showed me the move He wants to bring, I saw swift and eruptive moves of glory that led to mass deliverance. I was swept into a vision and saw entire stadiums filled with people. Suddenly God's glory came, but it was fire and glory. It knocked people to the ground, and demonic bondage was broken under the weight of His kingdom!

I believe it! I believe God has a plan for you. I believe God has a plan for your family. I believe God has a plan for the freedom of nations and generations. I believe God is unveiling the mysteries of destiny to a generation. Just as Jochebed was entrusted to birth something special, so are we in our time being entrusted by God to birth His special plans. We are invited to come up higher into His honor and glory. We are being invited to partner with His plans for our day. We are being invited to move in His majesty and experience His magnificent power. We are being invited to arise and fulfill our destiny. *Let's go for the glory!*

PROPHETIC PRAYER

Father, I thank You for freedom in the glory! I decree that I am set free when I come into Your glory. Your glory breaks down barriers, removes burdens, and brings strength into my life. I see and discern the operation of Your glory. I fight and win in the midst of Your glory. Your glory empowers me for victory, in the name of Jesus. Amen.

MY DECREE OVER YOU

I decree victory in the glory for you! I see kingdom plans and revelation being released to you as the brilliance of God shows up in your life. You are moving in greater glory and freedom. God has anointed you to live in His presence and experience His weighty authority in your life. I decree a realization of the glory of God upon you, within you, and through you, in the name of Jesus. Amen.

POINTS TO CONSIDER

- I must learn to walk in the glory, move in the glory, fight from the glory, and prevail with the glory.

- I find my freedom, purpose, destiny, and all God has for me in the glory!

Appendix

CONFESSIONS

HONOR

The wise shall inherit glory: but shame shall be the promotion of fools.

—Proverbs 3:35, kjv

Thank You, Lord, that I am an honorable person.

I decree that I live honorably.

I honor You, Lord.

I honor Your ways.

I inherit Your glory because I choose to honor and submit to You.

I confess that I honor my leaders.

I honor Your word.

I honor Your plans.

I honor Your ways.

I honor Your will in my life.

I honor Your vessels and those You have placed in authority over me.

I confess that my words are honorable.

I confess that my actions are honorable.

I confess that my heart is established in honor and my steps are honorable.

Thank You, Lord, for honor and integrity in my life.

I decree that I love righteousness and truth.

I love Your Word and Your ways. I cling to You and to Your truth, God.

PROTECTION

You are my hiding place; You will preserve me from trouble; You will surround me with shouts of deliverance.

—PSALM 32:7

I decree that I walk in divine protection.

My vehicle is protected.

My travels are protected.

I decree angelic protection.

I decree supernatural protection.

My family is protected.

My money is protected.

My assignment is protected.

My mind is protected from the thoughts of the enemy.

Thank You, Father, that the hosts of heaven protect me.

Thank You that the blood of Jesus protects me.

Thank You that my home is protected.

My home is a place of peace.

My home is filled with the glory of God.

No weapon formed against me prospers.

I run to You, Lord, in times of adversity!
You are my hiding place. I am safe in You.

TIMING

A man's heart devises his way, but the LORD directs his steps.

—PROVERBS 16:9

Thank You, Lord, for divine timing.
I decree that I move in the timing of God.
I decree that my steps are ordered.
I decree that I wait upon the Lord.
I am renewed in the waiting.
Faith and patience are working in my life.
I am not ahead of God or behind. I am right on time.
I move at the speed of the Holy Ghost.
I walk in Holy Ghost timing.
I walk in precise timing.
I am led by the Spirit of God.
God is working even when I don't feel Him working.
I trust in and rely upon God and His direction for my life.

LAUNCH

For neither from the east nor west, nor from the wilderness comes victory. But God is the judge; He brings one low, and lifts up another.

—PSALM 75:6–7

My promotion comes from the Lord.

He launches the right plans in my life at the right time.

I decree God's promotion in my life.

I decree God's exaltation in my life.

I follow God's plan, timing, and wisdom for my life.

I do not want the promotion of man; I want the promotion of God.

FAVOR

For You, O Lord, bless the righteous man [the one who is in right standing with You]; You surround him with favor as with a shield.

—Psalm 5:12, amp

Thank You, Lord, for divine favor.

Favor is upon my life.

Favor is upon my family.

Everywhere I go favor manifests.

I am surrounded by favor.

I have favor with God.

I have favor with man.

Favor is working for me.

Favor is opening the right doors.

Favor is closing the wrong doors.

Favor is causing the right people to like me at the right time.

Favor is causing my influence to grow.

Favor surrounds me like a shield.

I expect favor everywhere I go.

Favor is mine!

GLORY

Then Moses said, "I pray, show me Your glory."
—Exodus 33:18

Lord, show me Your glory!

I want to see, know, and experience Your glory.

Thank You, Lord, for Your glory in my life.

I carry the glory of God.

I value the glory of God.

I experience the glory of God.

I expect the glory of God.

I love God's weighty glory.

I love God's brilliant glory.

I love God's healing glory.

I love God's revival glory.

I love God's golden glory.

I expect unusual dimensions of the glory of God in my life.

Everywhere I go the glory of God goes.

I expect God's glory and goodness in my life.

I decree that glory is my portion.

I was made for the glory of God.

I am being transformed daily from glory to glory.

DELIVERANCE

If the Son therefore shall make you free, ye shall be free indeed.

—JOHN 8:36, KJV

I am a deliverer!

My life is a platform for the freedom of Jesus to show up and manifest in the lives of others.

I am not ashamed of the ministry of deliverance.

I hate the devil and demons.

I hate demonic strategies and attacks.

I decree that I am free.

I am free in my mind.

I am free in my body.

I am free in my finances.

I command all bondage to be broken.

I command all demons to flee, in the name of Jesus.

I release freedom in every area of my life.

Thank You, Lord, that You have set me free!

TRAVAIL

The LORD shall go forth as a mighty man, he shall stir up jealousy like a man of war: he shall cry, yea, roar; he shall prevail against his enemies. I have long time holden my peace; I have been still, and refrained myself: now will I cry like a travailing woman; I will destroy and devour at once.

—ISAIAH 42:13–14, KJV

I love prayer.

I love to birth Your plans and purposes, Lord.

I decree that I give birth to Your plans and assignments.

I pray until the breakthrough comes.

Thank You, Lord, for the ministry of intercession in my life.

I discern and recognize divine moments of prayer.

I am not afraid to look foolish in Your presence.

I am not afraid to give birth and travail.

I am honored to be able to pray what is on Your heart.

Thank You, Lord, that I am sensitive to prayer burdens.

FIRE

The hair on His head was white like wool, as white as snow. His eyes were like a flame of fire. His feet were like fine brass, as if refined in a furnace, and His voice as the sound of many waters.

—REVELATION 1:14–15

Thank You, Lord, for Your fire in my life.

I decree the fire and glory in my life.

I decree cleansing fire.

I decree holy fire.

I decree fire and awakening.

Thank You, Lord, for a fresh baptism of fire in my life.

I carry Your fire in my belly.

I decree that my life is a living sacrifice.

I clearly hear Your voice in the midst of the fire.

I live and walk in Your fire.

AWAKENING

Therefore He says: "Awake, you who sleep, arise from
the dead, and Christ will give you light."

—Ephesians 5:14

Anoint my eyes with eye salve.

I decree that I have fresh prophetic vision and insight.

*I decree that the spirit of slumber has no place in my
life.*

I command the spirit of slumber to be broken off me.

I release personal revival and awakening.

I say that I am a forerunner.

I love the love of God.

I have God encounters.

I am a burning one.

I experience regular renewal in my life.

*I decree fresh fire, fresh passion, and fresh moves of
God in my life.*

I move with God!

NOTES

Chapter 1—What Is the Jochebed Anointing?

1. Bible Study Tools, s.v. "prophet," accessed March 26, 2019, https://www.biblestudytools.com/dictionary/prophet/.

2. *Merriam-Webster*, s.v. "patient," accessed March 26, 2019, https://www.merriam-webster.com/dictionary/patient.

3. Bill Johnson, *Manifesto for a Normal Christian Life* (self-pub., Bill Johnson Ministries, 2013), Kindle.

Chapter 2—The Mystery of Honor

1. *Merriam-Webster*, s.v. "honor (*n.*)," accessed March 27, 2019, https://www.merriam-webster.com/dictionary/honor.

2. *Merriam-Webster*, s.v. "honor (*v.*)," accessed March 27, 2019, https://www.merriam-webster.com/dictionary/honor.

3. Bible Hub, s.v. "3513. *kabad* or *kabed*," accessed March 27, 2019, https://biblehub.com/hebrew/3513.htm.

4. *Merriam-Webster*, s.v. "protocol," accessed March 27, 2019, https://www.merriam-webster.com/dictionary/protocol.

5. Bible Hub, s.v. "1930. *epidiorthoó*," accessed March 27, 2019, https://biblehub.com/greek/1930.htm.

6. Bill Johnson (@billjohnsonBJM), "In the culture of honor we celebrate who a person is without stumbling over who they are not," Twitter, April 9, 2010, 2:26 p.m., https://twitter.com/billjohnsonbjm/status/11902081861.

Chapter 3—The Mystery of Protection

1. John Eckhardt, *The Prophet's Manual* (Lake Mary, FL: Charisma House, 2017), 135–136.

Chapter 4—The Mystery of Timing

1.   *Merriam-Webster*, s.v. "arrogant," accessed March 27, 2019, https://www.merriam-webster.com/dictionary/arrogant.

Chapter 5—The Mystery of the Launch

1.   Bible Hub, s.v. "5356. *phthora*," accessed April 3, 2019, https://biblehub.com/greek/5356.htm.

2.   *Merriam-Webster*, s.v. "launch," accessed April 3, 2019, https://www.merriam-webster.com/dictionary/launch.

Chapter 6—The Mystery of Favor

1.   Graham Cooke, "Training for a Life of Favor," *Brilliant Perspectives* (blog), accessed April 3, 2019, https://brilliantperspectives.com/training-life-favor/.

Chapter 8—The Mystery of the Glory

1.   Ruth Ward Heflin, *Revival Glory* (Hagerstown, MD: McDougal Publishing Company, 2013, 2018), 190.

2.   Matt Slick, "What Is the Shekinah Glory of God?," Christian Apologetics & Research Ministry, February 13, 2017, https://carm.org/what-is-the-shekinah-glory-of-god.

Chapter 9—The Mystery of Deliverance and Deliverers

1.   Derek Prince, *They Shall Expel Demons* (Grand Rapids, MI: Chosen Books, 2008), 19–20.

Chapter 10—The Mystery of Birthing

1.   William D. Mounce, Mounce's Complete Expository Dictionary of Old and New Testament Words (Grand Rapids, MI: Zondervan, 2006).

2.   *Merriam-Webster*, s.v. "atmosphere," accessed April 8, 2019, https://www.merriam- https://www.merriam-webster.com /dictionary/atmosphere.

3.   James Goll, "Travail: The Prayer That Brings Birth," *Elijah List*, January 21, 2005, http://www.elijahlist.com/words/display _word/2791.

Chapter 11—The Mystery of Protecting Emerging Seed

1. Bible Hub, s.v. "2032. *epouranios*," accessed April 4, 2019, https://biblehub.com/greek/2032.htm.

2. *Oxford Dictionaries*, s.v. "curse," Oxford University Press, accessed April 4, 2019, https://en.oxforddictionaries.com/definition /curse.

Chapter 12—The Mystery of Weakness

1. Charles H. Spurgeon, *Morning and Evening* (devotional), Heartlight Inc., accessed April 5, 2019, https://www.heartlight.org /spurgeon/0203-am.html.

Chapter 13—The Mystery of Temporary Decrease

1. Jack Hayford, *Seedtime and Harvest* (online devotional for May 1), Jack Hayford Ministries, accessed April 5, 2019, https ://www.jackhayford.org/teaching/devotional/seedtime-and-harvest/.

Chapter 16—The Mystery of Freedom in the Glory

1. Rebecca Greenwood, *Glory Warfare* (Shippensburg, PA: Destiny Image Publishers Inc., 2018), 190.

Ryan LeStrange is an apostolic and prophetic revolutionary, laboring to see global awakening. He moves strongly in the power of God traveling the globe to ignite revival fires and build a growing apostolic-prophetic movement. His conferences and gatherings are alive with prophetic declaration, miracles and healings, fire, and powerful preaching.

Ryan is the founder and apostolic leader of a global network of ministries known as TRIBE Network. He is a cofounder of AwakeningTV.com, a media channel created to host revival-inspired services featuring ministers and messages both past and present. He is the senior leader of the iHub movement, planting and overseeing a network of governing churches, apostolic hubs, and revival hubs. Ryan is also a real estate investor, active in the business arena.

Ryan is a best-selling author. His books include *Supernatural Access*, *Overcoming Spiritual Attack*, *Releasing the Prophetic,* and *Revival Hubs Rising*, which was coauthored with Jennifer LeClaire.

Ryan and his wife, Joy, have one son, Joshua, and currently reside in Virginia.

INVITE RYAN @ ryanlestrange.com

Instagram @ryanlestrange

Twitter @RyanLeStrange

Facebook.com/ryanlestrangeministries

Youtube.com/user/TheRyanLeStrange

Ryan LeStrange
M I N I S T R I E S
P.O. BOX 16206 | BRISTOL, VA 24209